Cricket & Beyond

CRICKET & BEYOND

Gulu Ezekiel

Ocean Books Pvt. Ltd.
ISO 9001:2008 Publishers

Cover photographs courtesy
Sachin Tendulkar and Brian Lara—Kamal Sharma;
Milkha Singh and Jeev Milkha Singh—Mohd. Shafiq

Published by
Ocean Books (P) Ltd.
4/19 Asaf Ali Road,
New Delhi-110 002 (INDIA)

ISBN 978-81-8430-100-7
Cricket & Beyond
by Gulu Ezekiel

Edition
First, 2011

Price
Rs. 250.00 (Rs. Two Hundred Fifty Only)

Printed at
Bhanu Printers, Delhi

To
My
Family

Acknowledgements

The author and publisher would like to thank the following for giving their kind permission to reproduce the articles published in this book:

Charlotte Atyeo (Jonathan Agnew's Cricket Year, published by A and C Black)
Mark Baldwin (ECB souvenir)
Richard Bath (Scotland on Sunday)
Adam Burnett (Inside Cricket/ACP Magazines)
Ivan Crasto (rediff.com)
Prabhu Chawla (India Today)
Indrajit Hazra (Hindustan Times)
Vinod Mehta (Outlook)
Chandan Mitra (The Pioneer)
Venu Palarpathi (dreamcrickt.com)
Satya Prabhakar (sulekha.com)
Anita Pujari, Priya Rai (DNA—Daily News and Analysis)
N. Radhakrishnan (Man's World)
N. Ram (Sportstar Weekly)
Mario Rodrigues (All Sports Magazine)
Prabhdev Singh (Golf Digest)
Aditya Sinha (New Indian Express)
Rob Steen (The New Ball)
K. Swaminathan (Namaskaar)

Foreword

I am delighted my friend Gulu Ezekiel is bringing out a book containing the 40 best articles from his past 30 years in journalism.

I have known Gulu for close to two decades and have always been impressed by his passion and commitment to sport in general and Indian cricket in particular.

His career has encompassed print, Net, radio and television and combined with this, the number of books he has written proves he is both versatile and prolific.

Gulu wears his passion on his sleeve and on the numerous TV debates in which we have featured together I have found we are on the same wavelength when it comes to issues and controversies concerning cricket.

This book contains an impressive array of Gulu's articles on a wide range of sports with an emphasis on cricket which is so close to Gulu's heart.

There are numerous articles on the India Premier League in this collection stretching back to its origins and the reader can judge for himself how perceptive Gulu has been on this vexing issue. On this we share common ground and many of our dire predictions on what we both consider a cancer in the game have proved uncannily correct.

Besides controversies, there is much to celebrate as well in this anthology and I wish both the book and its author all the best while looking forward to another such collection 20 years down the line!

—Bishan Singh Bedi

New Delhi
December 2010

Introduction

Such a long journey

No matter how many years you are in the business of journalism, the thrill of seeing your name in print never quite goes away.

The very first time was back in February 1980 in the magazine *The Weekly Sun*. Two years of freelancing later, I landed my first job in Madras. And twenty-one years after that first article, the wheel came full circle when I decided to go freelance again and also set up *GE Features* which has syndicated columns by Mahesh Bhupathi, Ajit Pal Singh, Shaun Pollock, Jacques Kallis and Sir Richard Hadlee.

The journey began in London in 1966 when aged just seven I sat enthralled in front of the TV with my elder brother and father as we watched England beat West Germany in the final of the World Cup football. And Wembley, the venue, was not far from where our family lived at the time.

Back in India, my passion for cricket like so many boys of that generation was ignited by India's twin wins in the West Indies and England in that magical year of 1971. Cricket has been the major factor in my life since then along with a fascination for the Olympics.

It was my father who instilled in my brother and me a love for sport. Dad was Bombay University champion in badminton and tennis and his trophies used to litter the house. My love for writing comes from my mother who even in her 80s has a passion for literature and poetry. So combining the two –sport and writing— seemed to be the logical thing to do.

I have written on numerous other subjects including space travel, science fiction, food, books, comics, music, Hollywood, Israel and the Middle East, international politics, religion, travel, sports stamps, adventure sport and humour. But sport and cricket in particular remain the bedrock of my career and that is why I stuck with that theme for this book.

Having completed 30 years of writing, I thought it was time to compile a collection of my favourite articles, mainly on cricket but other sports as well. In this I would like to thank my publishers, *Prabhat Prakashan* for their encouragement and support.

To maintain the integrity of the original text, I have not altered or updated portions mentioning contemporary records or events which may have changed since publication. I have also maintained the original headlines.

There have been many in the profession I would also like to thank for their inspiration and encouragement, starting with my first sports editor, late Olympian CSA Swami. And also all the editors who so kindly gave me permission to reproduce the articles in this book.

My guru as far as cricket writing is concerned is Anglo-Australian writer and historian David Frith, a father-figure to me who has encouraged me since my school days.

Bishan Singh Bedi is one of my all-time cricketing idols and is now someone I am proud to call a friend. I am truly honoured that he agreed to write the foreword to this book.

Since my freelance days, there have been some journalists who have proved to be a pillar of strength. Guys, I owe you.

To my family, friends and colleagues, a big thank you for making this journey such an eventful one.

—Gulu Ezekiel

gefeatures99@gmail.com

www.guluezekiel.com; gululuvscricket.blogspot.com;

Contents

Ramanathan—The Pioneer

This was and remains the most difficult interview I ever conducted. It was painful to see one of the legends of Indian sport in such a poor condition. Ramanathan passed away in 1990.

TK Ramanathan is a pale shadow of his former self. A month past his 76th birthday the father of Ramanathan Krishnan and grandfather of Ramesh Krishnan was bed ridden and weak when this interview was conducted. The words came out painfully and the memories had to be jogged along with help from Krishnan's wife Lalita who sat by Ramanathan's side throughout.

This then was the man who nearly 60 years ago was responsible for breaking down the social and national barriers that had been erected by the British rulers to keep themselves aloof from the 'natives', a man who started the line of one of India's foremost sporting families, who fought for his rights against enormous odds and showed the arrogant white man that Indians too were more than capable of holding their own on the sporting arena.

The life of Ramanathan is one of sacrifices, bold decisions and an unbending iron will to succeed. Both on November 3, 1910 in Tenkasi village in Nagercoil (about 400 miles from Madras), this stalwart of Indian tennis moved to Madras at the tender age of 18 in search of a job.

It was in 1930 that the first milestone in a noble life was passed when the 20-year-old Ramanathan paid a visit to the Madras United Club. Here he watched Madras No. one Bala Gopal in action. Thinking back all those years ago, Ramanathan reminisced: "I saw this puny man and thought to myself, if he can play, well, so can I." And thus unfolded the first chapter in a stirring saga of Indian tennis that continues till this day with the stirring of grandson Ramesh on the international circuit.

Of course for a young middle-class Indian to play tennis — that classic English gentleman's club game—was easier said than done in the India of the late '20s'. Apart from the discrimination prevalent, there was also the economic factor involved. Ramanathan made the startling revelation that he sold his wife's wedding ring to buy his first tennis racket–a Slazenger—for the grand sum of Rs. 34. "My wife has always been with me and made a number of sacrifices for my career," he emphasized.

Ramanathan first played the game at the Telegraph Recreation Club in Madras. No Indians were allowed to join and he had to get some high level recommendations before breaking in. Even then he was only allowed to play on the second courts which were meant for the inferior players.

The myth of inferiority was finally shattered in 1935 when Ramanathan beat all the top players in winning the club championship. "But even then, no help was forthcoming," Ramanathan recollects.

Ramanathan was forced to go to Delhi in search of some gainful employment and it was in the North that he began to catch the eye. After winning a tournament in Lahore, he claimed the Delhi State championship in 1938-39. The year Krishnan was born (1937) Ramanathan triumphed in the Mysore State championship.

Ramanathan was the first player from the South to gain a high National ranking, reaching number three in the country. He finished runner-up to the legendary Ghouse Mohammed at the 1939 all India Hard Court Championships but considers Iftekar Ahmed (who later immigrated to Pakistan) as the finest of his contemporaries.

World War II came in the way of Ramanathan's career. In 1939 he was to go to Wimbledon when war broke out and thus missed a golden opportunity. It would have been the only instance of three generations of a family playing there if Ramanathan had had better luck.

It was in Delhi that Ramanathan played a lot of tennis with the Viceroy, Lord Linlithgow. Ramanathan remembers with a touch of pride in his voice: "After I won the State championship, I got a call from the Viceroy's ADC inviting me to play. After that I was a regular visitor to the Viceroy's courts."

Talking of courts, Ramanathan said that in his opinion the South Club courts of Calcutta were among the finest of his time anywhere in the world.

Ramanathan recounted the story of how Krishnan became the first schoolboy to win the Stanley Cup tennis title at the Bertram tournament of Loyola Collage, Madras. Krishnan was a student of Ramakrishna School in T'Nagar. His father spotted in him early signs of greatness and in 1950, after seeing a notice in the papers fought with the Physical Director of Loyola College to allow his son to play, as it was then only open to college students. The authorities finally relented, thinking the youngster would not last beyond the first round. But Ramanathan's foresight ultimately paid off.

"The careers of my son and grandson were not accidental. I could spot their early potential. Their success was a result of hard work and natural talent."

Ramanathan took up coaching in 1954. Among his notable students, apart from Krishnan and Ramesh, were Lakshmi Mahadeven, Shanker Krishnan (Ramesh's cousin), Gowri, his grand-daughter and Ramesh's sister and V.K. Parthasarathy.

To build the court attached to his house Ramanathan sold all the land in his native place. "I consider it more a temple of tennis than a mere court," he remarked. Today the sand court stands as a mute witness to the days of former glory. As a coach Ramanathan said that a player needs hard work and natural talent in equal measures if he is to succeed.

As for the difference in the styles of his days and today, Ramanathan said players now put in more power and tend to make more mistakes as a result whereas earlier they were steadier and depended more on touch and artistry, for which his son and grandson are so famous.

Father and son were a well known doubles combination. They made their first visit to Wimbledon in 1952. Krishnan recalls how they went by train to Colombo and then embarked on an 18-day sea voyage, arriving at Marseilles, France and from there going to London by train.

"I remember arriving at Victoria Station and looking all around us with awe," said Krishnan, his memory still sharp after so many years. "We played as a pair in France."

"But coming from a poor family and without any support from them, we could only go thanks to a public subscription", remembers Ramanathan. How well that paid off, for two years later Krishnan was to win junior Wimbledon, his son Ramesh uniquely following in his footsteps a full 25 years later.

Ramanathan is now left with these memories in his old age. Perhaps they provide him with some strength. Well could he be known as the forgotten man of Indian tennis.

□

(New Indian Express, 11/12/86)

A Taste of Paradise on Earth

The visit to Sri Lanka was for a holiday. But like on most of my holidays, cricket and writing was never far behind

The Madras- Colombo flight is so short, it's over before you realise it has begun. But it does prepare you for a unique form of 'culture shock'.

A glance at the sports pages of the local newspaper sets you bolt upright in your seat. A full page is devoted to previews of the next day's school matches complete with banner headlines ('Battle of the Maroons'; 'Battle of the Golds) and photos of all the players. A phenomenon worth looking into, you think to yourself.

Nisal Seneratne, the manager of the Sri Lankan squad to the 1987 Reliance Cup tirclessly served as my liaison man with cricketers and officials throughout the week. His avowed aim was to arrange an interview with the President of the Sri Lankan Board of Control for Cricket, the Hon. Mr. Gamini Dissanayake, Minister for Lands and *Mahaweli.*

Seneratne, between taking periodic potshots at Indian grounds ("Pune and Kanpur where we played two matches in India are a disgrace and not up to Test standard. The outfield at Pune is uneven and the dressing-room facilities at Kanpur are very poor") and lauding the Pakistani centres ("they spent a fortune on modernising their grounds") did come out with some interesting observations on various aspects of the game in Sri Lanka or Ceylon, Serendip and Taprobane as it has been called down the centuries.

Yes, schools cricket is extremely popular drawing crowds of 10,000 and more and being shown on the National TV news but what happens after the jump from schools and colleges to the first class and international grade? According to Seneratne, a lot of talent is lost to the plantations.

A youngster from a prestigious college (the 'old school tie' syndrome is very much prevalent) is often snapped up by a tea company and spends the rest of his life as a prosperous planter. All further thoughts of cricket are forgotten.

The Minister celebrated his 46th birthday on Sunday (March 19) in the Capital. Seneratne assured me he would have wangled an invitation. But yours truly was spending a restful weekend on the hills of Kandy and Nuwera Eliya, an experience which is a must for any visitor to Sri Lanka. It was, after all, a holiday!

The next day was spent in a long vigil by the phone and in the hotel lobby waiting for good news from Seneratne. A case of 'all dressed up and nowhere to go'!

"The Minister is busy" was a sentence repeated often through the week. Indeed he is, being involved in the India—Sri Lanka Peace Accord.

It is apparently the norm is Sri Lanka to have Ministers as Presidents of sports associations. Mr. Dissanayake is also President of the table tennis body while Internal Security Minister Mr. Lalith Athulathmudali heads the badminton and athletics bodies, quite appropriately, as he proudly pointed out that he was the holder of the junior national record in the 110m. hurdles.

Consolation at not meeting the Minister came in the form of a visit to the Nondescripts Cricket Club--appropriately named--home of current skipper Ranjan Madugalle and also of the splendid indoor school of the Sri Lanka Cricket Foundation. The National squad was having its last workout before leaving for the three-nation tourney in Sharjah two days later. The only one missing was the skipper himself, who turned up a short while later, having skipped practice, being slightly unwell.

Madugalle, his country's fifth skipper in six years of Test cricket, and the youngest (at 27) on the current international circuit, must also rank as one of the friendliest, a characteristic of his people. In a short, informal chat, he discussed the problems facing Lanka cricket.

"Our main problem is lack of international exposure, Touring teams are reluctant to come here and we don't get many invitations. A player like Ravi Shastri who made his debut at more or less the same time as I has played four times as many Tests. I've played just two Tests this year and my next will be in England in August. Our younger players suffer most as a result, though they are very talented. Our local matches though of three days duration are not considered first class because they are not of an inter-zonal nature."

Madugalle was pleased with his team's form in the closing stages of the recent WSC one-day competition in Australia. "We really improved in the last five games which were close affairs and also beat New Zealand once. Our fielding picked up and attracted big crowds as a result of which the Australian Board made a profit on the tour".

Indeed, Aravinda de Silva finished just half a point behind David Boon in the Cricketer of the Year polls. Without actually mentioning Duleep Mendis and Roy Dias, both dropped from the side after six years. Madugalle did concede that his country was in the re-building process.

Ranjit Fernando came off the field, covered in sweat after giving his boys fielding practice along with fellow-coach Don Smith. Lanka's wicket-keeper-cum opener for many years before they were granted Test status, Fernando was in a nostalgic mood about Indian cricket. He was delighted to hear that the Indian veterans were playing in Pakistan and said that he was keen to have a veteran's teams from Lanka as well. But his first question was "Is Sivaramakrishnan still bowling?"

The news that Railways and Tamil Nadu were to meet in the Ranji Trophy final had Fernando recalling his many visits to Madras. He explained that he was raising the emphasis on the fielding "as this will raise the level of our bowling which is really quite mediocre. Our batting is our strength, but that's mainly on paper", Fernando added before excusing himself to join the team in its final 'rap session' in the indoor school.

Seneratne, never one to mince words, elaborated on the post Mendis-Dias era as it were. While Mendis is still active in local cricket, Dias was away in Zimbabwe leading the 'B' side. With the under-19 team in Australia (continuing their tour after the junior World Cup) and the senior team about to leave for Sharjah, there was a deceptively busy air about things. According to Seneratne, Mendis had put on a lot of weight ("apparently a family trait") and was very slow in the field during the Reliance Cup. "Remember Mendis was one of only four players to have played in all four World Cups. He's been with us for a long time and I doubt if he can make a comeback now. Dias still has a chance as he is younger."

Colombo is a small city in which everyone seems to know each other. Interest and knowledge of cricket is very high and even the layman can give you interesting tit-bits about the game. Not wanting to ruffle 'official' feathers, it was with a certain amount of trepidation that one broached the subject with the locals of the 'rebels' who had gone to South Africa in 1982-83 and were subsequently banned for 25 years.

What emerged was that it was certain disgruntled elements who were involved in the whole infamous episode, led by the manager of the team, former medium pacer Tony Opatha. The lure of 25,000 Pounds Sterling, in a country where foreign currency is so strong, was just too much for the players.

Many of them have gone into private businesses with what they earned. Sri Lanka's first Test captain, Bandula Warnapura for instance is running a rent-a-car company. Did I want to meet him? Yes, but then one was wary of opening old wounds which are yet to completely heal. "Some of the players were very popular and the whole episode was depressing for Lanka cricket," according to one knowledgeable local enthusiast with semi-official links with the game. Among the top players lost were Anura Ranasinghe, apparently captaincy material, Gary Wouters, a 'Burgher' (as is David Heyn, the flamboyant left hander who toured India in 1973-74) and wicket-keeper Mahesh Goonetilleke, who played in the Madras Test of 1982. For all of them, there will never by another game of cricket as they are banned at all levels.

Colombo boasts of three Test grounds, the latest one being an imposing 35,000 seat capacity stadium. But the country is blessed with numerous little grounds, all expanses of lush green turf. These dot the Galle Face Road which links Colombo with Kandy and Nuwera Eilya, adding to the spectacular scenery which has earned Sri Lanka the sobriquet of a 'Paradise on Earth'.

Despite all its troubles and strife that touch of Paradise is still not lost.

□

(New Indian Express, 31/3/88)

Yours Sincerely, Paul Whitelaw

Back in the days of 'snail mail' I had pen-friends from around the cricket world. But only one had a father who had played Test cricket and was a former world record holder to boot. This is the story of our correspondence.

It was in early 1981 that a common friend passed onto me the address of Dick Whitelaw from Auckland, New Zealand with the cryptic comment: "I think he's in some way connected with cricket."

The name struck a bell and on checking *Wisden* I noticed that a Whitelaw of Auckland had set a world record nearly 50 years ago. My curiosity whetted, I dashed off a letter to Dick. Sure enough, the former world record holder, Paul Erskine Whitelaw, was the father of my new friend.

Paul Whitelaw played for New Zealand as an opening batsman against Douglas Jardine's 'Ashes' winning team on their way back from the infamous 'Bodyline' series, in early 1933. It was considered one of those quirks of selection that he did not play more Tests. Those were the early years of New Zealand Test cricket, the nation having made its debut against the touring England team in 1929-30.

Although I had many questions to ask him, it was not until 1986 that I wrote to Dick's father. Paul Whitelaw patiently answered all my queries about his career in a long letter which I still treasure.

(The excerpts from the letter are in bold italics, while contemporary newspapers accounts sent to me by Dick, are in light italics.)

"You referred to my notable career and the notable word I question. I was just a Saturday afternoon cricketer as we all used to be here—better than some and not nearly as good as others..."

Not notable? Consider these figures. Paul Whitelaw played for Auckland from 1928 to 1947, scoring 2,379 runs (av.37.52) with five centuries. His two Tests yielded 64 runs at an average of 32. Against Wellington at Eden Park, Auckland, he became the first batsman to score a century in each innings in New Zealand first class inter-provincial cricket. And it was on New Year's Eve, 1936 that he and Willam (Bill) Carson added 445 runs for the third wicket for Auckland against Otago at Carisbrook, Dunedin.

It stood as a world record for the wicket until beaten by a Pakistani pair (Khalid Irtiza and Aslam Ali) 40 years later and is still the highest for any wicket in New Zealand first-class cricket history. Carson's contribution was 290 while Whitelaw hit 195.

Carson was to die of war wounds suffered in Italy in 1944. A top level rugby player, he had been awarded the Military Cross in recognition of his bravery displayed in the Battle of Mareth in Tunisia. He was 20-years-old at the time of his record.

"About the 445 stand with Carson—this was his triumph and I was just the guy at the other end. He got his 290 in a bit over four hours while I was collecting about half of his runs. He also became a soldier later on and unfortunately died of wounds while on the troop ship coming home. I was a bit luckier wounded only slightly in a different action but I still carry a bit of German mortar bomb deep in my leg."

'In making these (on-side) shots Carson showed splendid timing and a quickness of eye which made it possible for balls short of a good length and pitched on the wickets to be sent hard to square leg. His chief scoring strokes however were on the offside

between point and the bowler.

He got his 100 in 136 minutes 150 in 188, 200 in 210, 250 in 242 and his full score of 290 in 268 minutes. It can thus be seen how altogether attractive and delightful was his display.

Whitelaw, although much slower, played a particularly sound innings, and he, too, gave, bowlers and fieldsmen little hope during the whole day. He played strokes all round the wicket. His timing was perfect while, like Carson, he used his feet well to the slow bowling...Whitelaw got his 100 in 198 minutes, 150 in 273 minutes and his total 195 in 331 minutes...Carson hit 38 fours, Whitelaw 21 fours and a six' (The Dunedin Evening Star, Jan. 2, 1937)

Paul Whitelaw was 23 when he made his Test debut against England at Christchurch in March 1933. Harold Larwood had returned to England after his remarkable performance in the 'Ashes' series but the side had a formidable bowling attack consisting of Bill Voce, Maurice Tate, 'Gubby' Allen and Hedley Verity—I was particularly interested as to what Whitelaw thought of this legendary left-arm spinner.

"I batted against Verity in the Test in Christchurch, long enough to find out that he was good and then some. He sized me up pretty quickly and put in a silly mid-off. I tried to shift this back but being a bit slow footed didn't go down the wicket far enough for my drive and hit an easy catch to cover—out for 30. I played him again some years later (1937) in Auckland with much better results—99 not out. But getting back to this Christchurch Test, Voce with his many short leg fieldsmen, bowled at me. I handled him well enough to stay in for about an hour. At the other end, Tate gave me more trouble."

'Whitelaw and Dempster opened the innings against Voce and Tate. After lunch, Allen, the fast bowler, came on instead of Voce. Whitelaw handled the bowling rather better than Dempster. The field was placed for off-theory to both bowlers, but Allen had a deep fine leg, short leg and forward short leg... Whitelaw was out when he made a bad stroke in attempting a cover drive off

Verity, and was caught easily by Freddie Brown at extra cover. He had taken 75 minutes to get his runs' (N.Z. Herald, March 27, 1993)

The two Tests were noted for the mammoth scoring of Wally Hammond. In the first Test at Christchurch he hit an unbeaten 227 and then followed it up at Auckland with the-then world record of 336 not out, scored in 319 minutes with 34 fours and 10 sixes.

"I fielded while Hammond made 227… England made 560 for eight … We might have done bit better had we got Hammond out for zero at the start of his innings. He put one up in the slips out of reach of any fieldsman and so was not dropped – but think what might have been. In Auckland a week later he made 300-odd hitting several sixes one of which I might have caught if I had an extended arm of about 40 feet. But he was much too good for us, never looked like getting out and the drive was a treat to see. He appeared as good as we were led to believe."

Coming back to the innings of 99 not out (out of a total of 183) which Whitelaw considered probably his best ever, it was scored for a combined Auckland—Christchurch XI against MCC in 1937 just prior to the New Zealand tour of England for which he had been dropped. Verity and Ken Farnes, both of whom were killed in World War II, were the main bowlers for the tourists.

'Whitelaw placed his on-shots well and occasionally cover drove beautifully. One of the features of his innings was his solid defence. "It was a very fine display of correct cricket and I was very impressed with his sound defensive tactics," said England's captain 'Gubby' Allen' (NZ Truth)

In August I received an autographed photo from Mr. Whitelaw and sent a letter thanking him. The letter reached Dick on August 29. But a day earlier his father had passed away at the age of 78. He was cremated and his ashes were scattered over the main wicket at Eden Park, Auckland, scene of many of his triumphs.

□

(New Indian Express, 10/11/88)

A Paean to The King of the Square Ring

Since my childhood, Mohammed Ali has been one of my favourites sportspersons. I was fortunate enough to meet him in Madras in 1988. This was my tribute to Ali on his 50th birthday.

The 60's was all about power – Flower Power, Black Power and Ali Power. Mohammed Ali that is. For Ali was as much a child of and symbol of the Swinging Sixties as the Beatles, beat poetry and Carnaby Street.

On January 17 'The Greatest '—a self-proclaimed title that fitted like a crown on the king of boxing– completes half a century. And this is one birthday that the world will celebrate with both joy and more than just a tinge of sadness.

A few years ago it was discovered that 'The Greatest' had Parkinson 's disease, a debilitating ailment that affects the entire nervous system and slows one down.

The news was received incredulously by his millions of fans. Ail afflicted with 'Parkinson's? That would be like Fred Astaire losing his leg or Elvis Presley, his voice!

As far as Ali—and his admirers—were concerned, he was not only 'The Greatest', but also "the prettiest." Right through his 21-year career which involved 61 fights, Ali was never cut up badly.

For Ali's face and fists were his fortune.

That was something to do with his unique style of boxing. "Float like a butterfly, sting like a bee" became the man's anthem and trademark. The feet moved like greased lightning, the fists hit like thunder and the sum effect was tempestuous. The 'rope-a-dope' tactic was first tried out with stunning success in the 1974 title fight with George Foreman in Kinshasa, Zaire, the "rumble in the jungle." Rarely has a boxer been more favoured to win as Foreman was. Rarely has a boxer turned in a more masterly performance as Ali did that sweltering night. Forman slugged himself out and in the seventh round he collapsed like the proverbial sack of potatoes.

Immediately after the fight a tropical storm erupted. It was as if the gods themselves had broken into thunderous applause.

That was the only occasion in which Foreman and Ali would meet in the ring. But his three duels with Joe Frazier and Ken Norton were classics. And Ali claimed both 'series'2-1.

Whenever an Ali fight was due, it was as if the whole world was holding its collective breath. No sporting event this century has captured the public's imagination as the first Ali—Frazier bout held in Madison Square Gardens, New York in 1971. That marked the culmination of the greatest comeback in the history of sport, for it was after a fight involving one man against his own government.

The 'Thrilla in Manila' that followed four years later was one of the greatest bouts in boxing history.

The transformation of Cassius Marcellus Clay into Mohammed Ali, after he embraced Islam in 1964 was an event that rocked White America to its racist roots. From that day on Ali was a marked man. And when he refused to be drafted in for the Vietnam war, the full force of the establishment came down upon him.

The exile lasted 43 months, enough to break the will of lesser mortals. But never once during that harrowing period did Ali waver in his faith. That surely was his greatest victory.

It may though have tempered his brashness to a certain extent.

Having shocked the boxing world by snatching the world crown from the seemingly unbeatable Sonny Liston in 1964, Ali was not content to let his fists do the talking like the champions from the past. For Ali every fight was a showbiz and media event and he was the star. A mix of predictions and poetry—more like doggerels really–became another Ali trademark. And for years he would get it right, pinpointing the exact round in which his opponents would fall.

The only man who managed to seal the 'Louisville Lip' was Norton, who as a total unknown broke Ali's jaw in the first round of their 1974 fight. Incredibly, Ali dug into unknown reserves of courage to last the entire 15 rounds.

Sadly, like many fighters from the past, Ali never knew when to say goodbye. It would have been perfect if he had quit the ring after regaining the title for a unique third time when he beat Lean Spinks in their return encounter in 1978 at the age of 36.

Instead, he hung around for another three years and one of the saddest memories in sport was his pathetic display against Larry Holmes in 1980. Holmes, who would reign over the heavyweight scene for many years to come, spent more time pleading with the referee to stop the bout than using his fists. Holmes was a former sparring partner of Ali's and the fight probably hurt him more than Ali.

Sport has never been the same after Ali's departure. Neither Holmes nor Mike Tyson nor any of the others in between have been able to capture that special Ali magic.

Happy 50th , Mohammed. Here's to many more.

□

(The Pioneer, 171/92)

The Second Birth of South African Cricket

The early 90s was a fascinating and historic period both with regards to sports and politics. These were often inextricably intertwined as the case of South African cricket. This article was written on the eve of their first Test match after the apartheid ban was lifted.

When Mike Procter led the South African team off the field at Port Elizabeth on March 10, 1970 at the end of the series against Australia, he could scarcely have imagined that it would be the final Test of his brief career and his country's last for 22 years.

Procter had just taken 6 for 73 as the Springboks (as they were then called) completed a 4-0 whitewash of Bill Lawry's Australians, the same team which had just trounced India 3-1.

All South Africans rejoiced at the tag of world champions as they believed they were at the time. But the title had a hollow ring to it.

South Africa had never played Pakistan, India and West Indies in international cricket. The reason was the hated apartheid system perpetrated by the white-minority government. The policy saw to it that not one of South African's 235 cricketers in the country's 172 Tests were anything but white. Apartheid also ensured that the cricketers from the Veldt would face a long exile.

Despite the protests over the years by the country's supporters, the historical fact remains that the South Africans dug their own grave when the-then Prime Minister John Vorster refused to accept Basil D'Oliveira as part of the 1968 touring England team. 'Dolly' was a 'Cape Coloured' who had moved to England in the early '60s' and qualified to play for England since he had been rejected by the land of his birth.

The anti–apartheid movements in both England and Australia ensured that the proposed South African tours of their countries in 1970 and 1971 were cancelled. After years of an ostrich-like attitude, cricket had at last grown up to its responsibilities.

How times have changed. South African cricket will be reborn today at Bridgetown, Barbados after 22 long and often bitter years. A more unlikely venue could not be imagined for the historic moment. But thanks to the active backing of the African National Congress, led by Dr. Nelson Mandela, spiritual leader of the blacks and many whites as well, South African cricket is going through something of a renaissance as countries rush to invite the formerly shunned sportsmen to their shores. The formation on June 29, 1991 of the multi-racial United Cricket Board of South Africa was the turning point in the process of re-acceptance.

By a strange quirk of fate, Procter is very much involved with the current team as well in his capacity as coach. And so is Dr. Ali Bacher, the man who captained them in their last series in 1970. For over two decades Dr. Bacher has fought defiantly to keep South African cricket alive His methods may have been debatable, but it was always obvious that the doctor had the good of South African cricket at heart.

It was of course a pity that the world was deprived of seeing such fine cricketers as Graeme Pollock, Barry Richards, Procter and Eddie Barlow in action. Their careers were severely limited and later generations such as Vince van der Bijl, Alan Kourie, Denys Hobson and Garth Le Roux, among many others missed out altogether, having to settle for 'rebel' matches instead.

The world had its last glimpse of the Springbok greats during the World XI series against England and Australia which replaced the original series. Barlow, Procter, Richards and the Pollocks all dazzled, leaving cricket lovers with feelings of 'if only'. Fate and history had caught up with South African cricket.

The 'rebel' tours of the '80's were Bacher's brainchild. From the ground-breaking tour by an England side under Graham Gooch in 1981-82 to the disastrous series against Mike Gatting's Englishmen in 1989-90, the 'rebel' plans of Messrs Bacher, Joe Pamensky and Co. proved a constant nightmare to cricket's establishment, barely recovered from the ravages of Kerry Packer's WSC.

The South Africans even managed to lure the first non-white terms to visit the Veldt, first Sri Lanka and then the West Indies. Huge pay-offs were the country's answer to its isolation. But 'rebel' matches could never compare with the real thing: full fledged international cricket.

Historically speaking, the recent World Cup, where they reached the semifinals, was not South Africa's debut in a world competition. The first 'World Cup' was in fact the Triangular series held in England in 1912 between the hosts, Australia and South Africa, then the only three Test playing nations. South Africa fared considerably worse 80 years ago, losing all three Tests against England and two against Australia.

South Africa celebrated its Test Centenary in March, 1989. But it was a sombre celebration. Two years later they were making a historical tour of India. The change had been sudden and dramatic.

The first South African Test match lasted only two days. It was staged at Port Elizabeth in 1889, the same venue where 81 years later they would play their final Test before isolation set in. England won by eight wickets. For many years the South Africans were totally outclassed by England. But by 1905-06 they had won their first series, beating the MCC tourists 4-1.

Through South Africans have traditionally been served by pace bowlers of the likes of Neil Adcock, Peter Heine, Peter Pollock and Procter, it is off spinner Hugh Tayfield who is their highest wicket taker by far.

Known as 'Toey' because of his habit of tapping his toes on the turf before every delivery, Tayfield was a bowler of unerring accuracy.

The 1952-53 series in Australia was one of their finest. Under Jack Cheetham they drew 2-2.

The batting of Jackie McGlew and the bowling of Tayfield (30 wickets) were the highlights. Four years later the South African came back to draw 2-2 against England after losing the first two Tests on home soil.

The short but dazzling career of the left-handed genius Graeme Pollock took off in Australia in 1963-64 when he became his country's youngest centurion shortly before turning 20. It was also in the early 60's that Rhodesian Colin Bland stamped his class in the cricket world as arguably the finest out-fielder in the history of the game. Jonty Rhodes continues the tradition today.

Till the white-minority government was ousted in 1980, Rhodesia (now Zimbabwe) was part of the South African first-class structure and many of their cricketers played for the Republic, including John Traicos. The veteran off-spinner, the only player from the 1969-70 team still active in first-class cricket, was in fact born in Egypt.

On their last tour to England in 1965, Graeme and elder brother Peter turned the Nottingham Test into a family affair. Peter took five wickets in both innings and Graeme stroked a dazzling 125 and 59 to help South African win the series 1-0.

The aura of invincibility was beginning to form when Australia were trounced 3-1 back home under Peter van der Merwe's captaincy. The all–round performance of wicket-keeper Dennis Lindsay has never been matched.

The last series for the Pollocks Procter, Barlow, Bacher and Richards (which was also his first) proved to be their country's greatest triumph. Barlow made two hundreds, as did Richards and Pollock. In the second Test at Durban, Pollock hit South African's highest score to date, 274 with 43 fours and a five. Pollock was to play only 23 Tests and his average of 60.97 puts him second only to Sir Don Bradman among those who appeared in more than 20 Tests. Australia's highest scorer in the series was Lawry with 83. Ali Bacher had proved to be an inspirational leader.

Fittingly, it was Bacher who caught Alan Connolly off Pat Trimborn on that fateful final day at St. George's Park to end the series. The Republic's finest hour preceded what would be their darkest period.

Kepler Wessels, Allan Donald, Peter Kirsten, Rhodes and co. will be picking up the threads of a proud sporting tradition when they take on the West Indies for the first time in an official Test match.

□

(The Pioneer, 18/4/92)

When Procter Polished Sobers' Shoes

As a young Indian cricket fan in the 70s, South Africa was like forbidden fruit. The longer their isolation due to apartheid, the more our fascination grew with their cricketers. Meeting Mike Procter and the South African national team on their historic tour of India in 1991 was thus a magical experience.

As India and South Africa battle it out in the epoch-making Test at Durban a good question is, do the South African cricketers themselves have any prejudices against non – Whites? I' m in a position to tell.

It all started the day the South Africans landed in New Delhi on the last leg of their historic tour a year ago. I had sought out manager and cricket supremo Aaron 'Ali' Bacher, who is Jewish, with the idea of inviting the Jewish members of the team to the local synagogue. Vice–captain Mandy Yachad, Bacher and his family and Joe Pamensky, the former strongman of South African cricket, as well as some of the accompanying supporters were only too happy to accept.

Call it divine providence, but the contingent were leaving on Friday night and Friday is the weekly Jewish prayer day. Gathering the group together in time (they were staying at two hotels) and taking them to the synagogue was a logistical nightmare. Anyhow, it was managed. A rapturous welcome was followed by prayers, speeches and tea and then the mad rush back to the hotel to pick up packed bags and go straight to the airport.

Bacher was embroiled in a controversy, having accused Indian bowlers of tempering with the ball. It was Sudhir Dar's delightful caricature of Bacher, magnifying glass in hand, peering at a ball Sherlock Holmes-style that got me on to the team's bus. As Bacher was entering the vehicle, I thrust the sketch forward with a request for his autograph. Bacher and his compatriots enjoyed the joke and my request to travel with the team to the airport was acceded to.

The next hour was the most exhilarating and challenging of my journalistic career. Exhilarating because I was sitting literally at the feet of my boyhood hero Mike Procter. Challenging because I was indeed hunched on the floor there being no vacant seats on the team bus.

As I got taking to Procter, other joined in and soon we were having a full-fledged discussion. It started off with the revealing anecdote of how Procter and Barry Richards, traveling with a South African schoolboy's team in England in 1963, wanted to see the West Indies--England Test at Lord's. They volunteered as dressing room attendants, and were sent to the West Indies' section. The two white South African schoolboys actually polished Garry Sobers' shoes and cleaned the pads and other equipment of the black cricketers Five years later, Procter was playing alongside Sobers and other non-white cricketers in the English county league and, thanks to his all-round skill, came to be known as the 'White Sobers.'

Jimmy Cook and Adrian Kuiper chipped in with their comments. They remarked that all South African sportsmen were against apartheid but were helpless to do anything about it. "We were trapped in the society in which we lived," they said. Had cricket helped in changing attitudes, I asked? Yes, replied the South Africans. Cook explained: "It made whites respect non-whites because of their skills and broke down mental barriers. The rebel tours played a big role in this, he said

I asked Procter how he had managed to retain his appetite for the game through those decades in the wilderness, when Barry Richards could not. "For me, the team I was playing for always mattered most. In any case, cricket came naturally to me," he replied. By now, skipper Clive Rice had walked up to where I was and spoke of how educative it had been for him to play alongside Richard Hadlee for Nottinghamshire.

The bus lurched in to the airport. I happened to be wearing the South African team tie, a gift from Bacher's son-in-law. The security man, thinking I was part of the group, waved me into the VIP departure lounge, allowing me a few minutes more with the team.

As I later walked out of the airport, my mind was a whirl of 'scoops'. The cold November air jolted me out of my trance. *The Pioneer's* Delhi edition was yet to be launched, the Lucknow edition was still to be revamped, and I had no paper to write anything for. □

(The Pioneer, 15/11/92)

A Long Journey from Hell to Law Courts

The fight for survival by table tennis champion V. Chandrasekhar is one of Indian sports' epic sagas, one I followed closely both personally and professionally when I was based in Madras. This piece was written shortly after Chandra had won his case for medical negligence. Today he runs a successful TT academy in Chennai and is married with a young son.

The phone call came at night, just as it was time to leave office after a long day's work. "Chandra has been admitted to hospital and has taken a turn for the worse. Check it out."

A quick call to the hospital and an appointment was arranged for midnight.

The cloak and dagger manner of the doctors at the hospital aroused my suspicions. But they sought to put me at ease. Yes, complications had arisen during the operation but Chandra was fine and would soon be discharged.

What I did not know was that at that very moment Chandra was in fact still in a deep coma, struggling for his life. It was to be the start of a long and agonising struggle.

Chandra had been complaining of pain in the knee for sometime and finally decided to undergo arthroscopic surgery, something quite common for sportsman, for knee cartilage tear. The operation was performed on September 14, 1984. Several complications arose during and after the surgery and for 26 days he was in a coma.

By the time he regained consciousness, the table tennis star was virtually a cripple, unable to look after himself and a pale shadow of his former robust self.

I first saw Chandra is hospital in mid-November 1984. It was a pathetic and heart-rending sight with tubes stuck into his body and a far away look in his eyes. At that stage, his parents were optimistic and there was even talk of his returning to table tennis soon.

The harsh realty was to dawn only later. The damage was permanent and now the struggle was to regain some sense of normality rather than playing again. For it was the cerebrum, the part of the brain which controls the nervous system and co-ordination which was damaged. Fortunately, the mental faculties were not affected.

The hard part came after Chandra was discharged from hospital in December'84. Reduced to a paraplegic, he looked hopeless. This was the stage when all of Chandra's legendary will-power and fighting abilities came to the surface.

Chandra has always been a gambler in life, on and off the table. Whether he was match point down or leading comfortably, it did not bother him. He always went for his shots. That style was to help him bag three National titles in-a-row.

It was also to help fight a much larger battle, the battle for his own life. For Chandra was a man who never gave up no matter how grave the situation may have been.

For some time, Chandra was like a drowning man clutching at straws. Who could blame him? All he wanted was to lead a normal life again. Was that asking for too much? Yoga acupuncture, Ayurveda, all were tried, but to no avail.

Almost a year after leaving hospital, Chandra was told about the revolutionary treatment carried out by Dr. Paul Cutler in Toronto,

Canada known as the Chellation Drip Treatment, a process of intravenous drip.

Chandra felt this was his best bet. But it would cost him Rs.6.5 lakhs. Could a table tennis player gather that much money? It became yet another challenge not only for Chandra, but for his friends and fans as well.

Official bodies were not of much help. But it was the general public which responded magnificently. Donations began to pour into our newspaper office from all over the country, ranging from Rs.10 donated by school boys from their pocket money to huge sums from companies.

A few fans even made a 'pilgrimage' to Madras to hand over money collected from their colleagues, armed with *prasad* from temples and good wishes and blessings. All for Chandra. Some unscrupulous elements even tried to make a fast buck out of it. The end result was a staggering Rs.9.2 lakhs.

Chandra left for Canada in February 1986 and made another trip the following year. Chandra is convinced the treatment has done him a world of good. Indeed, for those who have followed his struggle his improvement from 1984 till now is nothing short of miraculous.

Even today, Chandra is not normal. Probably, he never will be; his speech is slurred, gait clumsy and vision impaired. But the will and determination are steely as ever.

The money really comes as cold comfort. It can never heal the pain and agony of the last nine years nor bring back his glory days when he was the most exciting and successful player in the land.

Though he still retains his links with the game he loves so much through coaching, the nagging feeling persists that he could have achieved so much more when his career was cruelly terminated.

The clock cannot be turned back now. At most there is a sense of relief that justice has been done. Having led the battle from the front for players' rights during his active days, Chandra has now set a precedent for sportsmen in the law courts as well.

It is a saga of courage and tenacity. Of will power and determination. A saga that will be written in letters of gold when the history of Indian sport is recorded. For as the Bard would say "Here was a Man."

□

(The Pioneer, 27/5/93)

‘Kasparov was Incredibly Rude’

Vishwanathan Anand as a young man was a joy to interact with. My prediction at the end of this interview was slightly off—he became world champion for the first time in December 2000 just a couple of weeks after turning 31.

Strolling across the sands of Besant Nagar beach in Madras, a short walk away from the house where he lives with his parents Vishwanathan Anand is in a reflective mood. It is barely two months since he fought and lost the good fight against Grand Master Gary Kasparov in the finals of the Professional Chess Association (PCA) world championship in New York. And as he looks back on that momentous event, the local lad has about him the air of someone who tried his best, but fell short of the final mark. For the time being, however, if there was any trauma involved, it was obviously left behind in the Big Apple.

It isn’t easy living up to the reputation of being one of India’s finest sportsmen. Especially if you have just returned after challenging renowned chess legend Kasparov. So what if you could not win? The media surge remains at its peak, as is revealed outside Anand’s residence. A local sports photographer waits patiently for a session with Anand even as a Calcutta journalist fires a volley of questions at him. With characteristic humility the champ faces it all. His skills, after all, are not only confined to the chess board. He is articulate and media-friendly as well. Both qualities that go towards making a world-class player.

How confident was he going into the final? Says Anand: "There is always the risk of being over-confident when you are preparing to face a weaker player". He hastens to add self-effacedly: "Of course, I did not have that problem in the run-up to the final. Kasparov is hardly the kind of opponent you can be over-confident about playing." The two had met across the table before though never in the finals. But Anand asserts it made little difference to his pre-game mental set-up as Kasparov had played with the advantage of white for 90 per cent of their previous meetings. As for Dutch psychologist Albert Toby, Anand clarifies he was present in New York more as a friend and someone Anand could talk to rather than for any professional reason.

Kasparov is rated as the world's greatest exponent of chess, someone who has stood unchallenged for 10 years now. Drawing the first eight games must have been something of an achievement for the challenger. "Well, the idea was not to push anything early. Just get settled and wait since it was going to be a marathon tie. That worked according to plan."

About opinions from experts that the advantage had swung in his favour at that stage Anand chuckles ruefully. "Grand Masters tend to go for sound bytes when analyzing games. Even I have done that on occasion," he says, gamely acceding to our photographer's request to clamber onto a catamaran parked on the beach. "I know this may sound funny coming from the world runner-up, but I feel my game still requires more depth."

The challenger's opinion on the king and his giant ego? "I don't think Kasparov wants to be seen as arrogant, its' just a matter to being super confident. But Kasparov, the chess player, cannot separate himself from Kasparov the human being." In that respect feels Anand, Kasparov and American genius Bobby Fischer share some traits. Chess is the be-all and end-all of their existence. "You bring to chess facets of your personality and what you are. I have interests other than chess, like music and world and current affairs. I also have many friends around the world with whom I like to keep in touch."

Perhaps it is the very fact that Anand is not one-dimensional and tunnel-visioned which makes him that much more sore over Kasparov's petulant reaction to his stunning defeat in the ninth game." I remember after winning that game I told the chief arbiter that I had pulled the whiskers of a tiger." It rang true. Kasparov did return with a roar. And in more ways than one.

"Till then we were polite and courteous to each other. But in the 10th game he turned incredibly rude. What was the need to slam down pieces and bang the door every time he went in and out of the room? His behaviour was atrocious. Ironically, he had the upper hand early in the game and there was no reason to act in that manner". And though Anand asserts he returned to normal by the end of the game, he still holds the view that players should have more respect for one another.

Back home, Anand expertly juggles the attention he attracts from journalists, hordes of whom seem to have descended upon him at the same time. Anand's parents, who have contributed in a major way to his growth as a player, have to be gently persuaded to join their son for at least one photograph. Mr. Vishwanathan, however, firmly puts across the point that they do not wish to share in the media attention that their son is garnering.

What of the future? Anand plans to continue playing both in the FIDE and PCA world cycles. He is currently taking a break though not for long before returning to tournament play in 1996 when he will participate in three events in the year. "Nigel (Short) took a rest of six to seven months after losing to Kasparov. But I do not want to get too rusty," he reveals. The next challenger cycle is after all barely two years away and Anand is surely the wiser and richer for the New York experience.

And talking of riches, just how much did Annad earn from his match against Kasparov? The PCA had decided two months earlier that 10 per cent of the earnings of both the winner (US $1 million) and the runner-up (half of that) would lapse into their coffers. This fact, however, was revealed to the press just before the end of the tie. While that and the 40 per cent which was deducted as US federal taxes (as well as various expenses) cut heavily into his share, Anand says there was still "something substantial" left and he had no complaints on that score.

Despite losing in the world final, Anand does not consider himself the second-ranked player in the world. "In a sense there is no such thing as a number two. Even the number one slot is uncertain. This is because the position may vary throughout the year depending on the points we claim in various tournaments, much in the way of the professional tennis tour. Gata Kamsky, Short, Anatoly Karpov... there are many of us slotted together."

The time is already running out for the interview and so is Anand's patience. ("It never takes just five minutes to take photographs.") Yet he complies gracefully to answer the final question: what does he think was the vital difference between the challenger and the champion? "Mainly experience. He has been much better prepared over the last 10 years. Since he is exempt from playing the Candidates matches (to decide the challenger), he does not have to show his game-plan while I have had to open my preparations to others in these matches. And finally, while he is used to finals of 20 games, for me 12 games is the maximum I have played. Chess is a game after all, where the mental and physical aspects complement each other."

"What am I doing here? Let's forget about chess." Anand admits this thought crossed his mind once too often when he sat across Kasparov making moves that ultimately proved too costly. They however remained brief flashes of frustration. New York is history. Anand's 26th birthday is round the corner. December 11 to be precise. Chances are he will be world champion before he turns 30. And that should be history of a different, much sweeter kind.

□

(Outlook, 13/12/95)

How Sachin Ticks

Apart from my books on Sachin Tendulkar, I have written innumerable articles, mainly for the UK and Australian media. This was my second article chosen for this series of books which ran from 1996 to 2002.

Ask Sachin Tendulkar if he has ever read a book and he will tell you he does not have the time. The last one he read must have been in school. Considering he was playing cricket with the 'big boys' in Bombay's tough school of knocks by the time he was 11, you can be sure studies were considered a necessary evil.

He did admit though that someone had loaned him a copy of Mike Brearley's *The Art of Captaincy* and he had read "a part" of it. (Judging by his captaincy record, he probably did not get beyond the photo captions.)

Fair bet then that Tendulkar has never heard of Jack Fingleton. Don Bradman of course is a hero for every Indian cricket fan and cricketer even when they start playing the game in their backyards or on street corners. Amazing really since the Aussie marvel never played a match in India.

Naturally enough the Indian media went bananas when Bradman revealed in 1996 that Tendulkar at the crease reminded him of his own batting, something confirmed by wife Lady Jessie. And two years later Sachin and pal Shane Warne were the only non-family members to get an audience with The Don himself in Adelaide on his 90th birthday.

But back to 'Fingo'. Opening batsman in the 'Bodyline' series, habitual Bradman-baiter and author of the classic, *Brightly Fades the Don*, the cricketer-cum-journalist once made the startling revelation about this *bete noir*: "bowlers bowled to him the way he made them."

More than 50 years after that insight, Tendulkar revealed to an interviewer that he too toyed with the bowler's psyche.

"It's about reading the bowler's mind," said Tendulkar. And while anticipation was important, he claimed the previous 4-5 deliveries gave him an idea on what to expect from a bowler and how to react.

"It's not just that I expected him (the bowler) to do this. Sometimes I compel the bowler to do this. I play in a particular fashion intentionally so he does something and I am prepared. And because you are ready, it looks like you had a lot of time."

Only once has he admitted to feeling nervous before an innings. Understandable really. It was his debut Test at Karachi and at the age of 16 he was facing a Pakistan attack comprising of Imran Khan, Wasim Akram and Waqar Younis (another debutant).

He candidly conceded he did not have a clue with Akram whizzing the ball past his head. Four bouncers in a row. The butterflies were flying around in formation in my stomach, he said years later with a laugh.

It was no laughing matter though for the kid in a man's world back in 1989.

"It was very tough and I thought I was not going to ever play Test cricket again. At times, I was beaten by pace, the ball went past my bat before I had completed my shot. I made 15, then a half century in the next match. After that Test I don't remember being troubled by pace as such."

Ironically, it was Imran who admitted he was troubled bowling bouncers to someone he considered a mere child.

India—Pakistan cricket is certainly not a place for the faint-hearted, especially not for callow teens.

In the fourth Test of that debut series, Tendulkar was hit smack on the nose by Younis. Blood gushed out, the physio rushed out—and was waved back—and the imperious Pakistan captain showed a tinge of compassion by advancing to the boy's aid.

The batsman would have nothing of it. A hankie was fished out to stanch the flow of blood. The next two balls left the fielders rooted as they were imperiously dispatched to the boundary.

It taught him a lesson for life and remains the only time in his career he has had blood drawn while batting.

"It was a good thing that on my first tour I got hurt on the nose. I realised that there could be nothing worse than that. There have been worse injuries than mine. But that gave me more confidence and allowed me to be aggressive in my mind. Even if I broke my nose, I decided on staying there and not being bothered about fast bowling," he said in an interview in 1996.

When the Old Master met the two Modern Masters in Adelaide in August 1998, Tendulkar and Warne were more nervous than they had ever been on a cricket field.

Once he had overcome his sense of awe, Tendulkar managed to ask Sir Don a couple of questions—what his movements were before the bowler delivered the ball (fast bowlers—back and across; spin bowlers—initial front-foot movement, though not commitment) and secondly, what his mental preparations were before a match.

The answer to query number two stunned the young man. It was office work between 7 to 10 in the morning, go to the match (often tossing still dressed in office wear) and then after the day's play, back to work.

Tendulkar's 'office' of course is the cricket ground. It is a full-time 'job'. Indians play more international cricket then anyone else. And unlike many other 'superstars' in the team, Tendulkar makes it a point to play domestic cricket whenever available.

Asked to describe his batting, he has said: "mine is a floating technique. Sometimes the balance of the body weight is on the front foot and sometimes on the back foot,"

Long-time Sachin-watchers (there are hordes of us out there) will tell you that he is always first to arrive at the nets and the last to leave. This is his laboratory, where he experiments, often simulating match conditions.

He has also been spotted on occasion batting and bowling left handed, fluently at that. He does everything with his right hand in everyday life—except when it comes to writing.

The 1998 Test series in India against Mark Taylor's mighty Australians was hyped as the Warne v Tendulkar show.

Practicing at the 'nets' in his neighbourhood club in Mumbai prior to the showdown, Tendulkar's preparations consisted of getting some local leg spinners to bowl to him on a pitch where the area outside the leg stump had deliberately been roughened up. It held him in good stead.

He warmed up for the three-Test series with his maiden first-class double ton, playing for Mumbai against the tourists. And though the hype initially got to Tendulkar, he proceeded to give Warne the hiding of a lifetime both in that series and in Sharjah right after that.

In 2001 when there was a return series, (later known as the 'greatest series ever') he was denied a century in the first two Tests.

Preparing for the third and final one at Chennai (formerly Madras), he had leg-spinner Sairaj Bahutule (who made his debut at Chennai) and veteran L. Sivaramkrishnan use similar bowling tactics as in 1998. He got the ton in the first innings.

It was under coach Ramakant Achrekar that he learnt the lessons of hard work. By the time he was 11, he would be at the 'nets' for five hours and more per day during school vacations.

Often, he would play in two club matches on the same day. If he was out early in one game, he would hop onto his coach's scooter and dash across town to play in another. At home he would hang a ball in a sock and practice his strokes against it in front of a mirror "thousands of times every night."

The cliché "eat cricket, breathe cricket, sleep cricket" must have been invented for Tendulkar.

Achrekar, who also coached Vinod Kambli told me that the left-hander score more runs at school level. "But he did not have the dedication or perseverance like Sachin and also developed bad habits. Sachin on the other hand always had a very sensible attitude and a strong family background, especially with his father and brother Ajit always behind him."

There was a short period, between 1992-94 when Kambli was outscoring his great school chum. It would take Tendulkar ten years to record his first Test double century. Kambli did it twice in his first four Tests. In One-day internationals too, Kambli was years ahead of Tendulkar in getting his first ton.

A friendly rivalry developed between the two. But it did not take long for the younger one (by a year) to race away with all the honours.

When I asked Ajit Wadekar ('cricket manager' of the team from 1992-96) the difference between the two, with a wry smile he merely pointed towards his head. Point taken.

The Indian team has often been referred to as a one-man army. It is easy to understand why. Rivals know that to get Tendulkar out is to remove the heart and soul of the team. His departure has such a demoralising effect, the rest of the batting often folds up.

On the other hand, a dominating knock from him has the effect of lifting the spirits of his teammates.

Lifting the spirits of the whole nation too. Tendulkar is one of the few genuine heroes left in the country, someone whose appeal is nation-wide, cutting across all differences. To say that cricket is the one unifying force in India is not an exaggeration.

The pressures? Think of David Beckham—and multiply it by at least a hundred. For Indians he is Tiger Woods, Michael Jackson and Barry Bonds rolled into one.

The population crossed a billion a couple of years ago. Millions more are scattered across the world in the Great Indian Diaspora. Many of them are connected to cricket back home via the Internet and cable TV. Just check out how many websites are dedicated to Tendulkar—there are hundreds.

Ask him about the pressure of other's expectations and he will shrug it off. Occasionally though the truth gets through. "Every time I got in, every innings I play, they (his fans) want a hundred from me. It is humanly impossible to live up to such expectations." This admission came at the end of 1998, his 25th year and his *annus mirabilis.*

In 1999 his father died the night before a crucial World Cup match against Zimbabwe in the World Cup. India had lost their opening match against South Africa and were desperate to open their account.

He flew home to Mumbai, performed the last rites and took the next flight back in time for the team's third game against Kenya.

The India—Zimbabwe match was in progress while he was in mid-air. A steward relayed over-by-over scores to him. The team's morale was shattered when they were given the news on the morning of the match. They were beaten in the final over.

There was a weird mix of emotions among his countrymen when the news of his father's death spread. There was a shared grief for their favourite son (and brother). "Would he be back" was the question on everyone's mind (though not lips) which no one (not even manager Anshuman Gaekwad and captain Mohammed Azharuddin) dared to ask was.

He was. Days after his father's funeral he ensured there would be no hiccups against Kenya. The century—the first on the 10th day of the tournament—may not have been his best in terms of the strength of the opposition. But he ranks it right up there for obvious reasons.

At the end of the match viewers were left to wonder as to who would burst into tears first—the Man of the Match or the man interviewing him, Tony Greig. (They both managed to hold back).

Watching the innings on TV, the words to Billy Joel's song *Pressure* kept ringing in my head.

Occasionally it does get the better of him.

"I cried so much when I was out, I could not see. The entire team consoled me. I could have worked my way to the century. I suppose I got carried away, wanting to take on the bowler. "

That was in Napier in 1990 when he fell 12 runs short of one of the few records that could never be his again—youngest to score a Test century. He was two months shy of his 17th birthday. The record at that time was in the hands of Mushtaq Mohammed (17 years and 82 days). The next series was in the summer in England. It would be too late by then.

By 1997 he was captain after being appointed the year before. It was not a happy period—he admitted he could not sleep before a match—and he was sacked at the end of the year. Neither was the second stint from 1999-2000 much fun. The job had been thrust on him much against his wishes.

The Indian team has an appalling record abroad. Right through they 90s they won just a solitary Test away from home.

That looked to be changing on the fourth morning of the third Test at Bridgetown. Set 120 for what would have been only their third win in the Caribbean, the batting crumbled to 81 all out.

Back in his hotel room, an Indian journalist was shocked to see him break down and weep. Captaincy has been one area of cricket that he has not been able to crack. There could be a third stint in the near future.

Ego? Pride? You bet. No bowler is allowed to get on top for a sustained period. That thinking was behind the assault on Warne in 1998.

He remembers every Test and One-day International innings (he is due to play Test number 100 and ODI number 300 on the 2002 tour of England), the bowler and the mode of dismissal right from the first innings at Karachi in November 1989. Every knock is studied on video. He can take you through them, stroke by stroke.

That dreadlocked opera singer-cum-fast bowler, Henry Olonga learnt a lesson at Tendulkar's hands in his golden year of 1998.

In a league match at Sharjah, Olonga surprised the batsman with a short ball that had him fending to slip. Out for 11 and India were beaten by Zimbabwe.

The two teams made it to the final that was to be played two days later. Those two days were spent at the 'nets'. He was determined to overcome that slight.

He did. India won by 10 wickets, Tendulkar's 124 not out was his fastest 100 (in 71 balls) and Olonga's figures read 6-0-50-0. He had taken four wickets just 48 hours earlier.

"Yes, I wanted to prove a point. You can get me out once like that, you can take me by surprise, but it's not going to happen everyday." The message was sent out loud and clear.

There is a new ego battle being waged in Indian cricket these days. This one is between 'The Man' himself and the one they are calling the 'new Tendulkar', Virender Sehwag.

The Bangalore Test against Nasser Hussain's Englishmen in December 2001 saw Tendulkar tested by the negative line bowled by left-arm spinner Ashley Giles (shortly to be outlawed). Time and again he padded away balls bowled outside the leg stump into the rough, often using his backside too.

Sehwag came in and promptly demolished that line of attack. Tendulkar's pride was piqued. He took 12 off an over from Giles and then in the next one jumped out and was stumped for 90—the first time in 89 Tests he had been dismissed thus.

Zimbabwe's left-arm spinner Ray Price—better known as the nephew of golfer Nick Price—got his bit of fame in the series played in India in early 2002.

He got Tendulkar three times out of three in the Tests. In the first at Nagpur Tendulkar ground out one of his slowest centuries. In the second at Delhi Price had him struggling in both innings. Sehwag meanwhile was smashing Price and the others all over the decrepit Kotla ground.

Bishan Bedi—one of the best of them all—has a theory that left-arm spinners have an advantage over short batsmen. He gives the examples of Hedley Verity and Bradman and Derek Underwood and Sunil Gavaskar.

So has a chink finally been found in Tendulkar's armour? International cricket's grapevine must be buzzing.

□

(The Best New Cricket Writing: The New Ball Vol. VII: Mind Games, 2002)

Willow Swingers Go for Graphite

Cricketers love their golf. But why? Below I attempt to analyse this relationship.

What is it about international cricketers and their remarkable obsession with golf?

Remarkable? You bet. Believe it or not, two former Test cricketers (Jim Burke of Australia in 1979 and England's David Bairstow in 1998) committed suicide because they had suffered injuries which would have prevented them playing golf after their cricket careers were over.

That's only part of the story of course. But it gives you some sort of an idea what a huge part golf plays in the lives of so many cricketers.

West Indies legend Sir Garfield Sobers is undoubtedly the greatest all-round cricketer of all time. But cricket was just part of his sporting prowess. He also represented Barbados (where he was born) in golf, football, dominoes (a competitive sport in the Caribbean) and nearly in table tennis and basketball too.

Of all these it is golf that is today his greatest love. He took to it seriously only after his retirement from cricket in 1975 by which time he was touching 40. Yet in a few short years he was captaining Barbados in the Caribbean inter-island championships (for the

Hoeman Cup) with a best finish of third and by 2001 his son Matthew had followed him into the team.

Still, it came as something of a shock to me when I read these words in his autobiography released in 2001: "If I had my life again I would be a professional golfer rather than a cricketer."

Ian Botham, Kapil Dev, Geoffrey Boycott, Herschelle Gibbs, Desmond Haynes, Lance Klusener, Ajay Jadeja…the list is endless.

But the man widely considered to be the greatest cricketer/golfer of all time is England's dynamic captain of the '60s, Ted Dexter.

"No matter how well he [Dexter] performed, there was always something missing for him; it was never quite 100 per cent…he was beyond perfectionist," says Sobers in his book.

Once when they played together Dexter shot a 68 at Wentworth, "a round of which any professional tour player would have been proud." But the following day he went to a pro, Clive Clarke for a lesson because he had missed a shot.

Dexter, author of two sporting novels 'Testkill' (on cricket) and 'Deadly Putter' (golf) competed on the European amateur circuit in 1978 at the age of 42 and was edged out from a place at the Open championships in St. Andrew's on a sudden-death playoff. During a challenge match, he was tied with Gary Player over 18 holes at the time when the South African was one of the world's top golfers.

Another former England captain, Boycott emphasized to me the other day in Delhi just how good Dexter was. "I stepped on a golf course for the first time as a youngster on my very first tour, to South Africa in 1962. Ted [Dexter] and I were paired against two English journalists. I did not have a clue. But my captain guided me at every hole and we won the match."

So does being a cricketer help when swinging the golf club instead of the cricket bat?

Boycott feels it is quite the opposite. And he is supported by the greatest batsman of all time, the late Sir Donald Bradman, one of the earliest cricketers to seriously take up golf.

It was in England in 1934 while recuperating from a serious illness that he first tried his hand at it. According to Bradman, golf did not affect his cricket, but rather the other way round. "There is a tendency to bend the left arm and slice the ball over the 'covers' which is a splendid method of getting in the rough", he was quoted as saying.

"I don't believe being a cricketer can help in golf, certainly not for a batsman", says Boycott, one of the all-time great opening batsmen. "Maybe it's easier for bowlers, but for a batsman the way the bat is handled and the way a golf club is swung is totally different."

Boycott was known for his single-minded dedication as a cricketer. He is a determined golfer too. But even he would find it tough to ever shoot a score less than his age.

Bradman achieved the rare feat in 1988 at the age of 79 with a 76 to win the A-grade medal at Kooyonga golf course off the championship tees. He was still shooting in the 90s into his late 80s.

Our very own Kapil Dev may very well surpass Dexter on the golf links. Though he first started playing only in 1995, it has now become an all-consuming passion. There is rarely a single day when he cannot be found at the DGC.

Now his ambition is to represent the country at the amateur level and his chance may come in the next Asian Games in 2006, by which time he will be 47-years-old. But that does not deter him.

"I really believe I have a chance to play for India and I am going to put in some serious practice to make it a reality. That's my next goal in life. I am not getting younger and this is probably my last shot at it," he says.

"This is a beautiful game where you are your own umpire. You have to keep going and always remember that if you cut corners you will be letting yourself down."

His only regret is that he did not play golf earlier. "I wish I had picked up golf while playing cricket. I would have scored at least 2,000 runs more."

The last word must go to Gibbs, South Africa's dynamic opening batsman who was banned for nine months in 2000 for his role in the match-fixing scandal.

"I enjoyed the break. It gave me the time to play more golf."

Obsession indeed!

□

(Golf Digest, Nov. 2003)

Very Very Special Laxman

VVS Laxman has long been a favourite batsman of mine. This is my tribute to his artistry.

From the selfish cricket fan's point of view you could say that India has plenty of doctors but few middle order batsmen as stylish and solid as Vangipurappu Venkata Sai Laxman. The world of medicine's loss has no doubt turned out to be cricket's gain.

His parent's (both doctors) decision in 1992 to allow him to skip his medical entrance exams despite excellent grades and instead send him to a national Under-19 camp in Bangalore can now with 20/20 vision be looked back at with immense satisfaction.

"I decided to give myself four years to make it in cricket, knowing that if I didn't, I could always go for medicine" he had said.

Sure enough, within four years he was making his Test debut with 51 against South Africa at Ahmedabad in November 1996.

An alert uncle spotted the infant Sunil Gavaskar in the maternity ward after a mix-up with a fisherwoman's baby and a young Sachin Tendulkar was sent to a cricket coaching camp to keep him out of mischief after he fell from a tree when he was 10-years-old . It was a close call for Laxman too.

The propensity for big hundreds was first noticed in an Under-13 match for Hyderabad in 1987 when the youngster scored 153. And the habit has stayed with him right through. Indian cricket can thank its lucky stars for those gifts of patience, concentration and stamina for they have enabled him in the last two years to be at the forefront of two famous victories over world champions Australia.

Still, the adjectives one hears most often when cricket writers and commentators struggle to find words to describe his stroke-play are 'stylish' and 'elegant'.

The roots of these aesthetic qualities of batsmanship can be traced to his home city of Hyderabad, more famous for the Charminar, *biryani* and the flamboyant Nizams but also home to the 'Hyderabad school of Indian Batting'.

While the 'Bombay/Mumbai School of Indian Batting' was traditionally attritional and orthodox (before Vinod Kambli and Tendulkar broke the mould), in Hyderabad it has always been about wristy, even flashy unorthodoxy.

Laxman himself had as one of his early coaches one of the original and most famous members of that school, the late Test batsman of the '60's, ML Jaisimha.

Abbas Ali Baig and Mansur Ali Khan 'Pataudi' also played a lot of their cricket in Hyderabad but the man who perhaps epitomized Hyderabad best was former captain Mohammed Azharuddin, who is still struggling to clear his name after the match-fixing charges of 2000 brought his career to an end after 99 Tests.

Laxman played a lot of cricket in Hyderabad with Azhar and some of that magic—the ability to turn balls outside the off-stump to the leg-side boundary with a mere flick of the wrists–must surely have rubbed off on the young Laxman.

Laxman has two triple-hundreds for Hyderbad in the Ranji Trophy. In an Indian side full of batting talent, he is the lone triple-centurion. And he almost repeated the feat in Test cricket too.

Out of 10 Test cricket–playing nations, only five have produced triple centurions. For nearly 20 years, Gavaskar's 236 not out against the West Indies in Madras remained the highest score for India. All that changed in one of the great turnarounds in the world of sport when India beat Australia after following on in the second Test at Kolkata in March 2001, just the third such occurrence since Test cricket was born in 1877.

That match is now part of Indian cricket's folklore as is Laxman's monumental 281, the highest score against an Australian side for 63 years. It moved former Australia captain Ian Chappell to dub him as 'Very Very Special' Laxman.

Just a year earlier the world champs had got their first taste of Laxman's talents when he blasted them for 167 from 198 balls in an Indian total of 261 in the third Test at Sydney. That was his first Test century and came at the end of a miserable series for the Indians who were trounced 3-0. And then at Adelaide last month it was his 148 in the first innings combined with Rahul Dravid's double century that once again took the wind out of the Aussie sails.

He is now the leading batsman in the world against Australia. In 10 Test matches he has scored 1,119 runs against the most formidable bowling side in the world with three hundreds (167, 281 and 148) at the phenomenal average of 62.16 against a current career Test average of 49.71 from 48 Tests (all statistics till the second Test at Adelaide).

By contrast, Tendulkar, long considered the champion side's scourge, has seen his average drop below 50.

There have been triumphs in the West Indies last year and South Africa in 2001 and more recently at home where Laxman saved India from the ignominy of defeat at the hands of New Zealand who had never won a series in India.

The bitterest blow though came when he was dropped fro the World Cup in South Africa. "I was very, very hurt" to be dropped he says. That was after just one failure on the disastrous tour to New Zealand late in 2002 where all the top batsmen flopped on the under–prepared Kiwi tracks.

It has been said and not without exaggeration, that he is not the quickest mover between the wickets or in the field and this must have gone against him when it was time for selection. Indeed in the recent final of the tri-series against Australia at Kolkata he floored four catches, thus almost single handedly handing the title over. And his run out ratio in ODI's is worse than even that of

Pakistan's lugubrious Inzamam-ul-Haq.

Test cricket though is where his talents have really flowered since he was promoted to the pivotal number three slot in the second innings of that epochal Kolkata Test after top scoring with 59 in the first innings. Till then he had been shunted from opening the innings to number six, a position he is now back at and comfortable with, as the masterly Dravid has regained his number three slot.

It was Laxman's 281 combined with Dravid's 180 that turned back the inexorable Aussie tide and made cricket history at the Eden Gardens.

It was Laxman and Dravid who came together at Adelaide to once again turn the tables on their fancied opponents, making them the only pair in cricket history with two 300-plus partnerships against Australia in Test cricket.

Both on and off the field they are a study in contrasts. Dravid–all technical correctness, Laxman–able to conjure up stunning strokes seemingly out of thin air with a mere wave of his magic wand.

In that sense they are reminiscent of another great pair of Indian batsman of an earlier era, Gavaskar and his brother-in-law GR Viswanath. The difference is that for some mysterious reason, Sunny and GRV rarely clicked together in a Test match.

Laxman is a vegetarian while Dravid is not. Laxman is a member of cricket's 'Discman Brigade' (the men who constantly listen to music with headphones) while Dravid is one of the game's great readers and his range of reading goes from the classic *To Kill a Mocking Bird* to motivational sport books.

India's famed middle-order is considered the strongest in the world, though strength on paper does not always translate into runs at the wicket. Tendulkar, Dravid and Sourav Ganguly were all born in 1973. Laxman will be 30 next November and is sure to be around for quite a few more years. Cricket fans all over the world can be mighty grateful for that.

□

(Man's World, January 2004)

Sub-plots in Sub-continent Add upto an Indian Stunner

There is still nothing quite like an India/Pakistan cricket match. Here I try to explain the magic to Scottish readers.

Mass hysteria has broken out in India and Pakistan with the first full tour by an Indian cricket team for 15 years. Work came to a grinding halt in offices and the streets were deserted as millions of fans in the two cricket-crazy nations decided the five One-day Internationals took precedence over everything else in their lives.

Though cricket has a massive following in Asia (Bangladesh and Sri Lanka being the other two Test-playing nations), nothing has matched the pre-tour hype surrounding these games.

The hype is a mixture of politics, religion, glamour and glitz and yes, even sport. The closest equivalent is perhaps football in Brazil.

India last visited Pakistan in 1997 for three ODIs while Pakistan played a full tour here five years ago. The last time India did the same in Pakistan was in 1989.

The violence-torn port city of Karachi was given just one ODI while the Indian players were guaranteed "Presidential-level" security. Still, there were still last-minute security concerns with

Indian Prime Minister Atal Behari Vajpayee finally giving his personal clearance.

With general elections in India slated for May, the ruling Bharatiya Janata Party was concerned a defeat in Pakistan would affect the mood of the people and their chances in the polls.

India have been playing One-day Internationals in Pakistan since 1978. But they had only won two matches before this tour and not a single Indian batsman had managed to score a century till Sachin Tendulkar's 141 in the second match at Rawalpindi last week.

Still, though it was greeted by mass jubilation around the country, the 3-2 verdict in India's favour was as per recent form.

It might be a different story in the three-Test series though with the first match starting at Multan on Sunday.

India's Test match record in Pakistan has been abysmal as they have failed to win a single Test on five previous tours. And though there has been an improvement since Sourav Ganguly took over the captaincy in 2000, India are yet to win a Test series outside of Asia since beating England 2-0 in 1986.

Still, they will be strengthened by the return to fitness of medium-pacer Ajit Agarkar and leg-spinner Anil Kumble who took all 10 wickets in an innings against Pakistan in New Delhi in 1999. Both missed the one-day series.

Though the Test series too will be keenly followed, it will not have the same mesmerizing effect on the fans as the One-day Internationals.

Stadiums in India and Pakistan are rarely full for Test matches these days while ODIs draw capacity crowds. India's victory in the 1983 Prudential World Cup in England followed nine years later by Pakistan lifting the title in Australia has ensured Test cricket takes a backseat to the one-day game.

Test cricket between the two nations was restored in 1978 after a gap of 17 years. This long break was bewildering to cricket followers in the West but easily understood by Indians and Pakistanis who had fought two wars in the period. Cricket was the last thing on their minds as the old wounds of the partition of India—which led to the massacre of millions and the subsequent birth of Pakistan in 1947— were re-opened during these conflicts.

In 1999 at the height of the World Cup in England the two nations were involved in a border conflict in the Kashmiri region of Kargil. Then in late 2001 India blamed an armed attack on the Parliament complex in New Delhi on Pakistan.

As a result cricketing ties were put on the backburner till Vajpayee and Pakistan President General Parvez Musharraf backed off from an eyeball-to-eyeball confrontation across the tense border through much of 2002 and began to talk peace once again.

This tour was thus seen as a diplomatic as much as a sporting breakthrough, all part of what the two nations like to refer to as CBMs (Confidence Building Measures).

The BJP, initially reluctant to clear the series, has already begun to spin political mileage out of India's win in the fifth and final match at Lahore, releasing a video with action footage of the game in the background juxtaposed with images of Vajpayee and a few words of appropriate inspiration.

Since the first series in 1952 there has been plenty of hostility from the crowds whenever India have toured Pakistan and vice-versa. India's captain K. Srikkanth was attacked by a spectator on the field of play on the first day of the first Test at Karachi in 1989 and many matches have been disrupted by unruly spectators.

This time however the thaw in relations has led to remarkable bonhomie between the thousands of visiting Indian supporters and their Pakistani counterparts.

"The spirit in the stands was unbelievable," according to Indian cricket fan Sumir Lal who crossed the border for the fourth and fifth ODIs at Lahore.

"Visiting Indian fans were in any case overwhelmed by the hospitality of the ordinary Pakistani on the streets, but in the stadium it went a step further — Pakistanis wanting to wave the Indian flag, wear Indian caps, and cheering lustily for every good shot by an Indian batsman."

Sport in this case at least perhaps does have the capacity to build bridges between nations and peoples.

□

(Scotland on Sunday, 28/3/04)

Karthikeyan in Pole Position to be India's First Global Racing Hero

There was a big buzz in sporting circles when Narain Karthikeyan became the first Indian to drive on the Formula-1 circuit.

Bernie Ecclestone is just discovering what the cricket world has know for nearly 10 years now—that India has a huge market for sports just waiting to be tapped.

The Formula-1 boss has promised to bring a race to India within three years. "India will definitely have a race. It's just a case of where." Hyderabad, Mumbai and Kolkata are currently the front-runners.

In a country of 1.3 billion, even 10% constitutes a massive number and India's burgeoning middle (and upper) class with loads of disposable income are considerably more than that—closer to 30% of the population.

It is this group that is tuned into elite sports like tennis, golf and Formula-1.

Cricket too had an elitist image. But India's victory in the 1983 Prudential World Cup in England, the staging of the World Cup here in 1987 and 1996 and the opening of the Indian economy to market reforms in 1991—coupled with the arrival of cable TV and the phenomenon of Sachin Tendulkar—changed all that. Today cricket is mass based and cuts across all strata of society.

Tendulkar, an avid Ferrari fan who says he has now switched allegiances to Karthikeyan's Jordan team will be in Melbourne on March 6 to watch the first Indian in a Formula-1 race. So will hundreds of his fans, mainly from Chennai (formerly Madras) in the southern state of Tamil Nadu where motor racing is the most popular.

On race days bars and luxury hotels in Chennai and many other big cities such as Kolkata, Delhi, Bangalore and Mumbai hold F-1 themed parties and are packed with fans cheering on their favourite teams.

Karthikeyan was born in 1977 in Coimbatore, an industrial city near Chennai. Coimbatore, where the major industry is garment manufacturing is considered the cradle of motor sport in the country. Both Narain's father, industrialist GR Karthikeyan (a former champion rally driver) and his late uncle Karivardhan were pioneers in this sport.

Having been born with a silver spoon in his mouth, there was never any lack of encouragement or funding for Narain in his early years. At 16 he left his home and joined the Elf-Winfield Racing School in France. Since then his focus has been exclusively on racing and today he enjoys the tag (coined by his sponsors) of "the fastest Indian in the world."

For the last five years Karthikeyan's followers watched anxiously as one opportunity after another to break into the elite group was lost as he could not muster the millions of dollars required.

This time his sponsors, the major backer being the multi-million dollar Tata Group of industries (based in Mumbai) helped him secure the berth. Much to the amazement of most Indians who are still trying to grasp the enormity of seeing one of their countrymen among the top 22 on the starting grid in Melbourne next month.

Though the response to Narain's elevation has been generally positive, even ecstatic, not everyone is over the moon.

One dissenting voice in the daily *Statesman* is Mario Rodrigues, author of the controversial book, '*Ranji: Batting for the Empire'*.

Backing Simon Barnes who warned of the perils of F-1 in India in a column in *The Times,* Rodrigues writes: "Karthikeyan's buyout of a slot in Jordan highlights the inversion of the First World-Third World relationship. While India may still be a supplicant nation in many respects, it has also become an important arbiter of the world's economic engine and the West and international institutions are looking for Indian funds to run or bail out its shaky institutions like Team Jordan or the F-1. The ICC [International Cricket Council] for example recognises this and genuflects before the might of the Indian market."

Karthikeyan is understandably sensitive about all this talk of his sponsors buying his way into F-1. "Those who think this is a marketing ploy do not know my history. I've won races in Formula Three against Takuma Sato and Jenson Button. It was about waiting for an opportunity", he said recently.

An editorial in the weekly *Sportstar* lauded his breakthrough. "Karthikeyan's entry into F-1 has turned out to be a watershed for the sport in the country. Representation in F-1 is a sure sign that a developing country has 'arrived' on the global sport market."

While his fans are not expecting any major surprises this year, it has been pointed out in the Indian media that some of the big names of F-1 including Michael and Ralf Schumacher and Eddie Irvine first got their break driving for Jordan.

India's roads are notorious for being among the most dangerous in the world. Indeed, Narain's worst accident did not happen on the track, it occurred near Chennai in 1999 while sitting in the back of his family car. A speeding truck smashed into it head-on and he was lucky to walk away with minor injuries.

Compared to that, driving on the world F-1 circuit could well be something of a cakewalk for Kumar Ram Narain Karthikeyan.

□

(Scotland on Sunday, 27/2/05)

Was He India's First Olympic Hero?

The story of Norman G. Pritchard and the campaign to ensure his two medals stay with India has been something of an obsession with me since the beginning of my career.

Seventy-five years after his tragic death at the age of 54, the legacy of Olympian Norman Gilbert Pritchard continues to haunt Indian sport.

Who was India's first Olympian? The first from Asia to win medals in athletics? And the first Indian, indeed the first Olympian to act in Hollywood movies?

Remarkably they are all one and the same person—but the Pritchard enigma is one of the biggest mysteries in the history of the Olympics.

Pritchard (born in Calcutta on June 23, 1875) enjoyed a long career in the Hollywood silent era of the 1910s and 20s, acting alongside such screen legends as Ronald Colman, Clara Bow and Gary Cooper.

But after decades of being an unsolved riddle, the key to the Pritchard mystery was unlocked by former Bengal Ranji Trophy captain Raju Mukherji unearthing Pritchard's stage and screen name while researching the Olympian's life and times with this writer.

Mukherji three years ago came across a review of Pritchard's most famous movie, *Beau Geste* (1926) in an old issue of the St.

Xavier's School alumni magazine where it was mentioned that the boy who studied in that famous institution in 1891 had changed his name to Norman Trevor on entering the world of Hollywood.

At his prime Pritchard was one of the world's leading athletes, winning silver medals in the 200 metres sprint and the discontinued 200 metres hurdles at Paris at the second modern Olympics to be staged following their revival at Athens in 1896.

Pritchard matched the best in the world at Paris, even setting a world record in the second heat of the 200 metres hurdles which Alvin Kraenzlein would erase in the final for his fourth and final gold of the Games.

The winning time in the final was 25.4 seconds with Pritchard second in 26.0.

The 200 metres was won by Walter Tewksbury in 22.2 seconds while Pritchard took silver in 22.8.

He also reached the final of the 110 metres hurdles (failing to finish) and besides participated in the 60 metres and 100 metres sprints where he failed to reach the finals.

Pritchard was also an outstanding footballer and was joint honourary secretary of the Indian Football Association from 1900-05 as well as the scorer of the first hat-trick in an official football tournament in India. He moved permanently to England in February 1905

The question though that has been nagging Olympic historians is whether he was representing Britain or India at the Paris Olympics.

India did not send an official contingent till the 1928 Amsterdam Olympics, though an unofficial team was sent in 1920. The first team from independent India competed at the 1948 London Olympics.

So was Pritchard taking part as an Indian or a Briton? His parents George Peterson Pritchard, an accountant and his mother Helen Maynard Pritchard were indeed British. But for 100 years his two silver medals had been credited to India.

It has to be emphasised here that till 1908 participants entered the Olympics as individuals rather than as selected members of a national contingent. Indeed the records of the early Olympics Games are haphazard and have never been given official status by the International Olympic Committee.

The standard reference book for the Olympics is David Wallechinksy's *The Complete Book of the Olympics,* first published in 1984.

Till the 1996 edition Wallechinsky credited the two silver medals won by Pritchard to India as had been the standard practice in all major reference books on the Olympics.

However, British historian Ian Buchanan came to the conclusion that Pritchard had represented Britain and published his findings in the January 2000 journal of the *International Society of Olympic Historians. (ISOH)*

This prompted Wallechinsky to take the medals away from India and award them to Great Britain in his 2000 edition. It was Buchanan who in 1997 discovered Pritchard's date of birth from *Thacker's Indian Directory* (under the Bengal parish registrar) in London.

Wallechinsky however told me he had "an open mind" on the issue and in the 2004 edition of his book he jointly credited the medals to both Great Britain and India.

Internet movie sites have the full listing of Pritchard's 27 movies (under his screen name of Norman Trevor), starting with *After Dark* in 1915 and ending with *The Love Trap* and *Tonight at Twelve,* both in 1929, the year of his death (of a "brain malady) on October 30 in Norwalk (now a part of Los Angeles). He also had a long career on the stage in Broadway that in the 1920s was more popular than the silver screen.

Dr. Bill Mallon, former president of the *ISOH* traced references to Pritchard/Trevor from the New York press of the 1910s and 20s, including his obituary in the *New York Times* issue dated November 1, 1929.

"National representation at the earliest Olympic Games is

controversial," according to Dr. Mallon," who also publishes a widely respected reference book on the Olympics. "But Norman Pritchard was a national of what was then called British India and I think his medals should be credited to India. This would make him the first Olympic medalist from India."

Though this has never been authenticated, legend has it on arriving in Paris in 1900 from London where he had been competing in athletics meets, Pritchard told the organisers he would like to represent the land of his birth. This is perhaps why for 100 years his two medals were credited to India.

At the height of his fame, Norman was one of the biggest names of the New York stage before concentrating on the new novelty to hit the US, talking movies.

A newspaper article dated February 18, 1917 recalls an incident that changed Pritchard's life. This piece also states that he shifted from Calcutta to the plantations of Assam at the age of 17 before coming to England with his father.

It was during a dinner in December 1906 in London (he had moved there a year earlier to trade in the jute market) in the company of his father that he was asked to describe the recent magnificent 'durbar' staged in Delhi to welcome Lord Curzon as the new Viceroy of India.

So dramatic and vivid was his description of the incredible wealth and opulence on display that he was mistaken as an actor by one Sir Charles Wyndham. Sir Charles invited the young Norman to take up a bit role in a play.

It was on the advice of Sir Charles that he decided to pay serious attention to his new found talent. This prompted him to eventually give up the jute business altogether and take up leading roles on the stage.

His final stage appearance was in '*The Captive*' in September, 1926. By then he had shifted his attention to the silver screen. But within three years his life came to an end under tragic circumstances as he spent his last few years in and out of mental asylums.

Are Pritchard's relatives still in the United States? His daughter Doris was single and in her 20s at the time of her father's death. It is not known if she married and had children.

It would be fitting if the Indian Olympic Association took the lead in establishing his identity as India's first Olympic hero.

□

(Sportstar Weekly, 9/4/05)

The Flying Sikh's Exploits

It is now a full half-century since Milkha Singh's agonising miss at the Rome Olympics. But the legend still endures.

Milkha Singh ranks as one of the greatest Indian sportspersons of all time. But his story is more than just about his sterling exploits on the track, culminating in the 1960 Rome Olympics where he missed a medal by a whisker in the 400 metres.

Milkha came to be known as 'The Flying Sikh' in an age where the sight of a Sikh in the West was still a novelty and where his flamboyant presence ensured him a large fan following.

But in 1947 the 12-year-old Milkha had just one mission—to escape to independent India with his life. His parents and other relatives had been massacred in front of his eyes in Lyallpur and Milkha was now literally running for his life, crossing the border at great peril.

All alone and with no one to turn to, athletics was to be his salvation and today if he is considered the living legend of Indian sport it is due to the grit and determination he showed in those painful early years. It was the Army that provided him with a refuge and all the facilities for his beloved sport.

Within a decade of his second 'life', he was making a name for himself on the international athletics circuit.

Two Asian Games, three Olympics and two Commonwealth Games...he left his mark far and wide.

In the 1958 Asiad at Tokyo, Milkha not only won his pet event, the 400 metres, he also beat the favourite in the 200 metres, the Pakistani Abdul Khaliq and was the toast of Asian sporting circles.

The same year at the Commonwealth Games (then known as the Empire Games), he won his favourite event in 46.6 seconds, beating the South African Malcolm Spence, a name that would come back to haunt him two years later.

He was peaking perfectly for the Rome Olympics as his name spread far and wide, making him one of the most famous Indians of his time.

He entered Rome as one of the favourites for a medal after an outstanding season on the tracks of Europe. Facing him was the greatest array of quarter-milers ever assembled.

Milkha drew the fifth lane in the final after the heats had seen the Olympic record equaled by the American Otis Davis. The Indian star had beaten all the top quarter-milers in the world in the run up to Rome, except Davis. The experts predicted at least a silver medal for Milkha who would later admit that even he had gold on his mind, such was his form at the time.

Milkha still remembers the race as if it were yesterday.

"Going into the stadium for the final, I was quite relaxed but when I saw my rivals, the tension mounted. And with each minute it increased. I drew lane five with South African Malcolm Spence to my left and the German Manfred Kinder on my right. I was going strong till about 250 metres. But then I slowed down a bit. I thought the pace was very fast and I would fizzle out in the end if I continued at that speed. At that point I even looked back or maybe it was just a side-glance. But that fraction of a second decided my fate. One by one they all caught up with me—Spence, Kaufmann and Davis and it was all over. My mistake will rankle within my heart till my dying days. I could not wipe out the deficit of those six or seven yards in the last 100 metres, though I was running at my best.

"I desperately tried to catch up with at least the boy in the third place (Spence) whom I had beaten in the Commonwealth Games. But he was caught up with the first two runners and it helped him. We crossed the finish line almost together. I knew I had made a crucial mistake but was hoping against hope as I waited for the official photo finish. But as my bad luck would have it, I was declared fourth even though my time (45.6) was better than the existing Olympic record of 45.9. Davis and Kaufman were both clocked at a world record time of 44.9 and Spence was third in 45.5."

This race is considered one of the greatest of all time with the first two breaking the existing world record and the third and fourth the Olympic record. Even the fifth and sixth place (Kinder and Young) who both clocked 45.9 broke the pre-Rome Olympic mark. It was that kind of race. But that was scant consolation for the heart-broken Milkha.

Unofficial automatic timings were also available at Rome and the timing for the winner was put at 45.07 seconds while Spence was third in 45.60 and Milkha was recorded at 45.73.

"My dreams were shattered", recalled Milkha with deep regret many years later. "I waited for the medal ceremony and congratulated Davis, Kaufmann and Spence. But to tell you honestly, I hated doing it. If I had my way I would have snatched the medals off their hands and run away."

It was not long before depression set in. "After the race, I had no interest in anything. I felt after years of dominating the sport that decline had set in. I passed a few days immersed in sorrow. To return to India in that state of mind would have been dangerous."

So instead Milkha did what he knew best. He participated in competitions across Europe to take his mind off the near-miss.

He returned to India wondering how he would face his supporters. He need not have worried. Back home he was received as a hero. Though his mistake rankled for years, gradually Milkha regained his confidence and composure.

Milkha was soon back to his winning ways, claiming gold in the 400 metres in the 1962 Jakarta Asian Games.

Milkha's national records (200 and 400 metres) have been broken after many decades. But nothing can diminish his towering stature. He now leads a contented retired life in Chandigarh after a stint as Director of Sports in the Punjab government. His son Chiranjeev 'Jeev' Milkha Singh is one of India's leading pro golfers. The sporting spirit of the Flying Sikh thus lives on in the next generation.

□

(Sportstar Weekly, 30/7/05)

Cyclone Dhoni

MS Dhoni was new on the scene when I wrote this article. A couple of years later I wrote the first biography on India's captain.

Adam Gilchrist has made life pretty tough for wicket-keepers, particularly in ODIs. It is no longer enough for them to stay alert behind the stumps for 50 overs; now they are expected to stand and deliver with the bat too.

The 'Gilchrist Effect' was seen at its best during the ODI between India and Sri Lanka at Jaipur on October 31.

First, Lanka's Kumar Sangakarra carried his bat for 138 not out. Then he had a ringside view as his counterpart Mahendra Singh Dhoni set the record for the highest ODI score by a 'keeper (beating Gilchrist's own mark), a blazing 183 not out which is also the highest score by a player batting second.

That barnstorming knock came the day before *Diwali*, the foremost festival in India which is like the local version of Guy Fawkes Day—loads of light and sound, though with a religious angle to it. No surprise then that he has already been nicknamed *'Dhamaka'* (Big Bang) Dhoni.

Three days later at Pune with India needing 12 runs to clinch the 7-match series, he was at it again—two consecutive sixes in the 46th over to make it 4-0 for the home side. This just a few months after smashing the Pakistani bowlers for 148 in only his fifth ODI.

Indian crowds just cannot get enough of him.

Dhoni says Gilchrist is his idol, though he admits: "I have a fair distance to go before I reach anywhere near him."

Dhoni in fact is hardly your typical Indian cricketer. Tall for a 'keeper, muscular and super-fit, his long hair dropping below the collar is dyed red, an Indian version of 'Funky' Miller.

Reportedly, shampoo brands are all set to sign him up and fortunately for them indications are it will be a long time before he heads to the barber. "It's only been a couple of years since I decided to go for long hair. I used to have short hair but the new hairstyle has brought me luck and I intend to keep it that way."

Both in physique and technique cricket's very own Samson comes closest to that prince of big-hitters, Kapil Dev. Like Dev, Dhoni too has his roots in a part of India that has never before produced an international cricketer. Dev was from the northern town of Chandigarh, while Dhoni is from the eastern town of Ranchi, better known till now for its steel industry and mental asylum.

For captain Rahul Dravid, the keeper/batsman's arrival has been a godsend. No longer will India's premier batsman have to double up behind the stumps in ODIs as he did during the 2003 World Cup.

Just don't call him a pinch-hitter. "I am a strokeplayer," Dhoni likes to emphasize. Coach Greg Chappell's move to promote him to number three in the batting order was just another of those things that seemed to click in the ODI series against the Lankans, the first that India have won at home in over three years.

Inevitably now, the talk is not if but when he finally breaks in to the Test side. The incumbent Dinesh Kaarthik must no doubt be feeling the heat and indications are that Dhoni will get his chance when the Lankans return for three Test matches in December.

"The emergence of Dhoni may prove to be the answer if he continues to develop in both disciplines," Chappell had commented a few months back.

Chairman of selectors Kiran More, a former wicket-keeper

himself, makes all the right noises about that impending elevation when he says Dhoni's "evolution augurs well for himself and the future of Indian cricket."

"I don't know when it will happen [a place in the Test side] but I'll wait for my turn," is all the man will say on the rather delicate subject.

There is also talk of Dhoni perhaps becoming the first to score a double century in an ODI. At Jaipur he came in at the fall of Sachin Tendulkar's wicket in the very first over. Another over or two and he could have reached the milestone. "I don't know about it but there is a possibility it would happen.

Somebody could do it. There are so many brilliant strikers like Sehwag, Shahid Afridi and Adam Gilchrist," he says.

The media scrutiny means we are now aware that Dhoni loves drinking milk, riding motor-bikes and playing computer games and is such a hero in his hometown that he cannot step out of his house without getting mobbed.

And yes, he did have a hair-cut once this year. We know that too because the photo of him sitting in the barber's chair with hundreds of fans jostling for a view was carried in almost every Indian newspaper.

Now just imagine the frenzy if he gets to that double century first!

□

(Inside Cricket, January 2006)

Bowling Them Over

Here I attempt to bust one of the enduring myths of India-Pakistan cricket tours.

Contrary to popular belief, bonhomie was not first introduced in India/Pakistan cricket when India toured in 2004. It is time recorded history set the record straight.

In recent years the first steps away from animosity between the two countries was taken by Chennai spectators.

In 1997 when Pakistan opener Saeed Anwar set a new world record for the highest score in ODIs (194) against India, the crowd rose to its feet in applause as soon as he reached the landmark.

Then two years later it was Chennai fans again that showed its sporting side after Pakistan won a nail-biting Test by just 12 runs. They overcame their dejection at the Indian defeat and gave the Pakistanis a standing ovation as they took an unprecedented victory lap around the MA Chidambaram stadium.

Such an act by either team had been unheard of in Indo/Pak contests and nor had fans in either country responded in such a manner to any form of success by the opposing team or an individual.

Just two years earlier an ODI at Karachi had to be curtailed as the Indian fielders on the boundary were being pelted by stones.

It was however the Indian hockey team that received the most hostile reception when they visited Pakistan for the World Cup in 1990. The Benazir Bhutto government sponsored large groups of violent spectators who made the championship a living hell for the Indian players, raising the Kashmir issue at every match. There were reports that the Indian players were even assaulted by hotel staff once they stepped out of their rooms.

Though the team flopped, they were awarded the Fair-Play Award by the FIH (International hockey association) as they stayed on in Pakistan despite intense provocation.

It was the Indian board that had backed Pakistan for Test status in the ICC. This was instrumental in Pakistan touring India for the first time in 1952, just five years after Partition.

Pakistan's stalwart opening bat Hanif Mohammed wrote in his autobiography: "We were met with such warmth and treated as family. Everywhere we went we were treated with civility…It was a credit to Indian hospitality. We were overwhelmed with the reception."

Another Pakistan legend, Fazal Mahmood wrote: "We enjoyed the Indian tour both on and off the field and were simply overwhelmed by the friendliness of people at the centres. They welcomed us with open hearts."

India visited Pakistan two years later, only to be met by a wall of hostility wherever they went. The manager (and former captain) Lala Amarnath recalled: "There was one single purpose—to break the spirit of the Indian team off the field so that it could tell on their performance on the field."

The Pakistan captain, AH Kardar in an inebriated state and in the company of three hefty assistants assaulted Amarnath in the hotel lobby in Lahore. The incident is vividly narrated by Rajender Amarnath in his marvelous book on his father.

When Test cricket was renewed in 1978 after a gap of 17 years, the visiting Indian captain Bishan Singh Bedi claimed his phones were tapped. His Pakistan counterpart Mushtaq Mohammed in his pre-series pep-talk told his players to treat the series like a 'jihad' while senior player Majid Khan—echoing the words of Zulfiqar Ali Bhutto—commented that "Pakistan is ready for a 1,000-years war with India."

This is not to claim that Pakistani touring teams have not been given a torrid time in India too. But Indian fans should be given credit for both setting the trend of friendship in 1952 and then breaking away from years of hostility first witnessed in Pakistan in 1954 and perpetrated in Sharjah till the '90s.

□

(Hindustan Times, 12/1/06)

How Cricket Bowled us Over

An attempt to unravel cricket's hold on the nation

Jeev Milkha Singh is hardly the first Indian sportsperson—and certainly won't be the last—to feel cheated by the unfairness of it all.

India's top pro golfer is making waves on the world circuit while the Indian cricket team is going through one of its periodic slumps, epitomized by the latest Durban drubbing.

But neither Jeev nor a host of other successful Indian sportspersons can make a dent in Indian cricket's massive edifice.

Perhaps Sania Mirza came closest last year when 'Sania Mania' swept the nation. Young, female, attractive, controversial and successful, she seemed to have cracked the code in 2005. But this year has seen a slump in rankings and a subsequent slide in popularity.

That success/popularity co-relation however mysteriously appears to leave cricket in India unscathed. Even the match-fixing scandal of the early 2000s barely made a dent.

Indeed, Bob Dylan's '*A Simple Twist of Fate*' could well be Indian cricket's theme song.

For luck/fate/fortune—call it what you will—has played a surprisingly major role in the rise and rise of cricket.

Chew on this: India won the World Cup hockey crown for the first (and still only) time at Kuala Lumpur in 1975. Some of us can still vividly recall hearing Jasdev Singh and friends go ecstatic—on the radio that is—as India beat Pakistan 2-1 in the final.

It was in 1982 that television came of age in India with the Government ushering in the colour and 'live' era on the grand occasion of the Asian Games in New Delhi.

And what a wonderful opportunity our hockey stalwarts had as they reached the final (against Pakistan of course), staged in front of the Capital's political and social elite.

The result? A 7-1 humiliation. It took the players of that hapless side years to get over the trauma.

Hockey's golden chance to capture the imagination of the nation was lost that dismal afternoon in New Delhi. And less than 12 months later it was cricket that cashed in with style.

Yes, no one gave us a snowball's chance in hell at the start of the Prudential World Cup in England and right till the semifinals we had to be content with AIR's commentary.

Then things began to go topsy-turvy. India took on and beat England in the semis before shocking the invincible West Indies in the final with Doordarshan relaying BBC's live TV coverage.

The final ended at midnight in India with those two mundane but epochal words plastered across the bottom of our screens—'India Wins'.

It was more than 'Kapil's 'Dev'ils' however who had won a match and a title; it was a triumph for Indian cricket as a mass movement. The victory prompted India and Pakistan to snatch the next World Cup from under the noses of the game's traditional powers, England and Australia and the second miracle was wrought four years later—the World Cup shifted to the sub-continent in 1987.

Nine years later it happened again and by the late 90s it was obvious that cricket ruled in India, on par with movies and the stock exchange—all three weaving dreams of riches, fame and grandeur in the minds of millions.

Indeed the second wave for cricket came in the early 90s as

fate once again brought together three movements that changed India forever—the arrival of satellite TV, the rise of Sachin Tendulkar and the opening of our markets to the world.

Dylan had struck again!

So what about poor hockey? It is realistic to assume that had there been TV in 1975 and had India won the 1982 Asian Games final, it would have been hockey rather than cricket that would be stomping all over other sports in India today, especially given its glorious history of triumphs till the '60s . And while Indian cricket post-1983 has had more downs than ups, there have been enough triumphs to sustain the passion.

As for hockey, second-last place at both the men's and women's World Cup events this year just about sum up how low the game has slipped.

Then again, Indian cricket is a big fish in a small pool of 10 playing nations (of which 2-3 barely cause ripples). Indian hockey on the other hand has to go through a grueling qualifying tournament before it can even make it to the World Cup proper—a small fish in a very big pool indeed.

It does not help that the Indian Hockey Federation is arguably the most inefficient sporting body around.

But here's the irony. Go to any local club hockey tournament in the country, particularly in the North and the stands will be packed.

It is the same case with club football in Bengal, Kerala and Goa and volleyball and basketball in rural areas of Tamil Nadu and Kerala.

Cricket's equivalent, the Ranji Trophy will not attract even a couple of hundred spectators. It's just One-day Internationals involving India that draws in the crowds and the media and marketing frenzy that goes with it.

And yet Indian cricket stands unchallenged in terms of money, fame, glamour and media mileage. No wonder all other sportspersons are left cursing cricket under (and sometimes above) their breath.

Vishwanathan Anand, Rajyavardhan Singh Rathore, Sania

Mirza, Dhanraj Pillai, Jeev Milkha Singh, Jayanta Talukdar, MC Marykom—champions all. Really though, does anyone care?

Unfair? Sure, but then in India at least life's a pitch!

□

(DNA—Daily News and Analysis, 25/11/06)

Padded Up for The Nation

Cricket has set a wonderful example to the nation when it comes to its secular spirit.

Our politicians may not have anything better to do with their time these days and so cricket-bashing is the flavour of the month currently in Parliament.

The Indian team touring South Africa is the target of the nation's ire. But it took a phone-call from an Urdu newspaper in Mumbai in the middle of last week's 'Debacle at Durban' to open my eyes to an aspect of Indian cricket that needs to be universally applauded.

"Is it the first time there are four Muslims in the team?" was the question. To which my answer was: "Please check the score-card of the very first Test match played by India at Lord's in 1932".

Mohammed Kaif, Munaf Patel, Wasim Jaffer and Zaheer Khan (Durban 2006)—Irfan Pathan had been dropped from the playing XI—are the spiritual heirs to the legacy laid down by S. Wazir Ali, S. Nazir Ali, Mohammad Nissar and Jahangir Khan (Lord's 1932). And four years later at the Oval in 1936 six of the Indian playing XI were Muslim.

The newspaper's headline the day after the Durban ODI: '*Hindustan one-day team mein pehlee baar chaar Musalmaan ek saath.*'

Yes, there is much wrong with India cricket. But while I have not done the necessary research in other sports, there is no doubt that cricket stands tall in India when it comes to treating our minorities in a fair and just manner.

Indeed that famous first Test team, captained by the legendary CK Nayudu, also had in the playing XI two Parsees and a Sikh.

Thirty-two out of 256 players who have represented India in Test cricket are from the Muslim community and four of those have been captain—Iftikhar Ali Khan (the Nawab of Patadui Sr.), Ghulam Ahmed, Mansur Ali Khan (the Nawab of Pataudi Jr.) and Mohammad Azharuddin. The percentage break-up is just about the same as the official figures for the community as a whole in India.

In addition, two Christians (Vijay Samuel Hazare and Chandu Borde), a Sikh (Bishan Singh Bedi) and two Parsees (Polly Umrigar and Nari Contractor) have also captained in Test matches.

More than 30 years after his retirement 'Tiger' Pataudi remains the most charismatic, idolized and romantic of our cricketers. He led without a break for an amazing nine years and then came back for one final glorious series four years after he had been sacked as captain.

Pataudi was the first captain to do away with the bane of regionalism in team selection. For Indian cricket's greatest weakness has not been religious discrimination but instead selectors chosen on a zonal basis who invariably back players from their own states.

As captain Pataudi always insisted on merit being the lone criteria for selection and Indian cricket under his leadership forged a united identity and character for the first time.

Pakistan's cricket fraternity has felt uneasy with the leading role played by Indian Muslims, though this appears to be changing in recent times.

When India toured Pakistan in 1978 for the first time in 18 years their commentators insisted on referring to wicket-keeper Syed Kirmani by his surname only.

According to a leading Indian cricket historian, this was because the surname is also common in the Sindhi community!

A passage from a book on Pakistan cricket, '*Pride and Passion: An Exhilarating Half Century of Cricket in Pakistan'* by Omar Noman (a former UN official and Oxford University lecturer) sums up this ambivalence.

When India and Pakistan played for the first time in 1952, Ghulam Ahmed, more noted for his off-spin bowling, helped to save the fifth Test at Calcutta with his batting and ensure India won the series 2-1.

Writes Noman: "The fact that Ghulam Ahmed was a Muslim added to the poignancy of his efforts. It was as if a Jew had scored a goal against Israel, playing for an Arab team."

Two Hindus and four Christians have represented Pakistan since that first series. One of those later converted to Islam and is now the leading batsman in the world.

But it was when Mohammad Yousuf was in his earlier avatar as Yousuf Youhana that a storm was raised after he briefly led Pakistan while regular captain Inzamam-ul-Huq was injured.

This did not go down well with some former Pakistan cricket greats who cast aspersions on Youhana's "character", leading London-based Pakistani cricket writer Kamran Abbasi to speculate on the character of some of the players who had earlier captained Pakistan!

Abbasi had also written in April 2004 how Youhana's chances of ever being appointed captain on a full-time basis were slim as some of his teammates "are shamefully reluctant to be led by a captain from a minority group."

All that has dramatically changed now and Youhana is already being talked of as Inzamam's heir-apparent.

It was only in India that cricket was played along communal grounds. The Triangular, later Quadrangular and finally Pentangular tournaments (stretching from 1907-8 to 1945-46) in Bombay in pre-Independence days were fiercely opposed by Mahatma Gandhi and sections of the Bombay press.

It is no wonder considering they pitted the Muslims, Hindus,

Parsees, Europeans and the 'Rest' (consisting in the main of Indian Christians, Jews and Buddhists) against one another in matches that drew huge crowds, but never any ill feeling.

Writing the foreword to a recent book on the tournaments, the late S. Mushtaq Ali noted: "I can say without hesitation that though the teams were divided on communal lines, they were all united in their love of the game and there was seldom any ill feeling between either the players or the spectators of different communities."

That spirit lives on in Indian cricket. Our politicians could well take a leaf out of Indian cricket's history books rather than periodically condemning it.

□

(Hindustan Times, 28/11/06)

India and The World Cup

This article was due to be published in the in-flight magazine of an airline. But the entire issue had to be scrapped after India's shock early exit from the 2007 World Cup in the Caribbean.

One-day International cricket came late to India. It was a decade after the very first ODI had been staged in Melbourne in 1971 that Indian fans had their first taste of the limited overs version of the game.

The Indian Board was in no hurry to introduce it. After all, Test cricket was still king, drawing full houses. And as for India's performance in ODIs, well…! The first World Cup in England in 1975 was a disaster from India's point of view and the second in 1979 was no better.

All that changed of course when India stunned the sporting world by winning the 1983 Prudential World Cup in England. And to think that before that epochal moment, our sole win had been against unknowns East Africa in 1975!

Snatching the World Cup from under England's noses and shifting it to the sub-continent for the first time in 1987 was a masterstroke by a Board not particularly known for its innovative and quick thinking.

There were plenty of skeptics, particularly in England and Australia who were convinced India and Pakistan would botch things up when they jointly hosted the Reliance World Cup in 1987. Instead, it turned out to be one of the best World Cups of all time, even if neither of the hosts made it to the final.

One of the biggest surprises of 1987 was the emergence of Navjot Singh Sidhu as a brilliant stroke-player. And what a treat he provided us in the opening game of the World Cup in Madras.

Just a year earlier India and Australia had been involved in only the second tied Test of all time. Now they would produce another thriller.

It was the first time Madras was hosting an ODI and the early morning rush and surging crowds remain an abiding memory. It was hard to get into the stadium, but once instead it was harder to take your eyes off the pulsating action.

In those early days of ODIs, a total of 250-plus was considered a challenging one and when Australia stormed to 270 for 6 from 50 overs, it looked like India would struggle.

Remember, this was the last World Cup to be played in traditional white clothing. No fielding restrictions or Third Umpire replays either.

The crowd was treated to a flurry of boundaries from the Indian top order with Sidhu smashing five sixes in his 73. Imagine the shock then when last man Maninder Singh was bowled by Steve Waugh with one ball to spare and India one run short.

It was déjà vu of the worst kind for Indian fans as a year earlier it was Maninder again who was last man out, allowing Australia to snatch a tie in the Test match.

No mandatory post-match press conferences either and as the Indian journalists crowded outside the dressing rooms, captain Kapil Dev refused to allow us to talk to Maninder. "He is crying!" we were told, though years later Maninder denied this to me.

After that early setback, India went from strength to strength and surged to the semifinals. If in 1983 it was a cocky England who were stunned in their backyard by dark horses India, this time it was the defending champions who under-estimated England. A huge cloud of gloom descended over the nation as the English batsmen swept their way to the final.

The final at the Eden Gardens between traditional rivals England and Australia remains the closest yet, going down to the final over. But it was like a party without the hosts as Australia had beaten Pakistan in the other semifinal in Lahore.

By the time the World Cup returned to India in 1996, the Asian bloc, led by a new, aggressive India was beginning to take control of world cricket. The traditional powers did not like it one bit and the run-up to the tournament was marked by acrimonious controversies.

If 1987 saw India go out at the hands of England, the Wills World Cup semifinal between India and Sri Lanka at Calcutta ended in tears—mainly shed by Vinod Kambli—and bitterness as the game was awarded to the Lankans with India on the brink of certain defeat. As the match slipped further and further out of India's grasp, the crowd grew restive, then riotous and ruined what had been a magnificent event till then.

There were ominous signs of things to come though. The opening ceremony at the Eden Gardens had turned into an expensive shambles. The celebrity announcer bungled his lines and the city was suddenly struck by powerful winds that wrecked all the grandiose plans. In the end, only Alisha Chinnai's foot-tapping live performance of '*Made in India*' saved the show.

The other portent came in India's penultimate group match against Sri Lanka in New Delhi. It was a stinging defeat at the hands of a team that was destined to win the title thanks to its dazzling array of stroke-players.

If getting into the ground was an early challenge to the Capital's cricket lovers amid chaotic scenes and flailing police *lathis,* what followed was hard to swallow as the Indian bowlers were being given a sound thrashing too.

Renovations were going on in the stadium right till the start of the match and the constantly swaying structures was mirrored by the jitters the Indians were suffering on the field.

The defeat meant India were to take on Pakistan in the

quarterfinals in Bangalore. The knockout nature of the encounter raised passions to fever pitch and all those witnessing the match will attest to the Chinnaswamy Stadium being a steaming cauldron of emotions.

In the end Sri Lanka saved Asia's cricket reputation and we all celebrated when they beat the mighty Australians in the final at Lahore. It was the closest a host side has come to winning the title, the Lankans being co-hosts with India and Pakistan.

The World Cup was back in England in 1999. But by now it was obvious that it was Asian spectators around the world who were supporting and virtually bankrolling cricket. England'99 was no different—no wonder it became known as the 'Asian' World Cup.

This time I decided to visit England for the two semifinals and final as a spectator and tourist rather than as a journalist and it gave me a new perspective after so many years of sitting in the press box.

Watching cricket in England is an altogether different experience from the sub-continent. The smallness of the grounds means crowd control is not an issue and crowd comforts and conveniences are much more pronounced. There is a carnival, picnic-like atmosphere at most of the venues and spectators can easily move around without being penned in by excessive security.

With India having been eliminated, it was also fun to watch as a neutral spectator without any of the tensions associated with backing your own side.

The first semifinal at Old Trafford between Pakistan and New Zealand was tame and one-sided with Pakistan romping home by nine wickets. The one aspect of the match I can still remember vividly was the terrible din maintained throughout the match by Pakistan's supporters!

My trip was made though by the next semifinal between Australia and South Africa at Edgbaston. Having had the privilege of watching only the second tied Test in history in Madras in 1986, I now found myself witnessing the only tied match in the annals of the World Cup!

Being seated near the boundary I found myself close enough to lean over and almost touch the fielders. Seeing a match from ground level was a new experience and a fascinating one as well. The smallness of the ground meant I had a 360 degrees vision of the play.

Those last frantic moments culminating in South Africa panicking and Australia snatching the tie under tremendous pressure was remarkable to witness first-hand. But the lack of an announcement over the public address system meant most of the crowd was unaware that Australia had reached the final thanks to having beaten South Africa in their Super Six encounter five days earlier at Trent Bridge. It was only the ecstatic reactions of the Aussie fielders that gave us in the crowd an indication of this result.

It seemed like every Londoner of Pakistani descent was clamouring for tickets to the final. Hundreds of them were milling outside Lord's on the morning of the final, pleading for tickets. I resisted the temptation when one desperate fan offered me 1,000 Pounds for my ticket that I had bought for 100!

I did not regret hanging onto it. The final was one of the most one-sided of all time. But freed of the rigours of reporting, I have to admit I spent more time wandering round Lord's soaking in the atmosphere—and spending a bundle on cricket goodies at the Lord's shop— rather than watching the action.

At the end of the game, the crowd spilled over onto the turf—another unique experience for an Indian cricket watcher—and applauded the awesome Aussies. Who could have guessed this would be the last time Steve Waugh would be part of a World Cup match?

Meanwhile, Indian fans will have to wait another four years for the World Cup to return here for the third time. It should be a blast.

□

(Unpublished, March 2007)

Brian Lara—The Flawed Genius

Brian Lara was one of cricket's most stylish players and also one of the great enigmas. This article was written during the closing stages of the 2007 World Cup, Lara's swansong.

Brian Lara had it all as a batsman—short, like so many other greats, light on his feet, steely wrists, exquisite timing, the eye of a hawk and the courage to play the most audacious of shots in the most exacting of circumstances.

What he lacked though was the ability to inspire his teammates and raise their own standards. As captain of the West Indies in three different stints, he was an utter failure. But in that category he was not alone—other legends like Garry Sobers, Sachin Tendulkar and Ian Botham to name just three were also found wanting when it came to leadership.

The World Cup being staged in the Caribbean was always going to be the grandest stage for Lara's swansong. But though the opponents on Saturday (England) and the ground (Kensington Oval in Bridgetown, the spiritual home of West Indies cricket) are ideal, how Lara would have dearly wished his exit had come a week later—in the final rather than in an inconsequential last Super 8 match.

Looking back in cricket history, the batsman closest in style to Lara must have been Australia's Neil Harvey. But for those of us not privileged to have watched that great left-hander, Lara provided a feast for the senses that lit up international cricket for 17 years.

Like other troubled sporting geniuses before him—football great Diego Maradona springs to mind—Lara had an equal ability to fascinate and infuriate. And on numerous occasions he managed to do both at the same time.

What made him stand out amongst his contemporaries was his ability to construct massive innings. Indeed, his maiden Test century was 277 against Australia at Sydney in 1993.

The name of Lara will forever be synonymous with the two biggest individual batting feats of all time.

It was at St. John's, Antigua in 1994 that he carved out 375 against England to erase the world record of 365 not out held by Sobers since 1958.

Then, less than two months later he astonished the world of cricket by becoming the first man to cross 500 in a first-class match. His 501 not out for Warwickshire against Durham at Edgbaston took him past Hanif Mohammed's 499 set in 1959.

It made him the only cricketer since Don Bradman to hold both records simultaneously.

But the year ended in turmoil instead of triumph. The sudden spotlight and riches that poured in proved too much for the lad from Santa Cruz, Trinidad.

"Cricket is ruining my life," he moaned and was on the verge of dumping county cricket and going back home to rest his tired body and withered psyche.

By now the enfant terrible of West Indies cricket was beginning to assert himself. He felt the captaincy belonged to him by right and led a revolt against the incumbent Richie Richardson at the 1996 World Cup that sabotaged the team's chances of reaching the final.

It would not be the first time Lara's petulance would get the better of him and split the team. His giant ego was spiraling out of control.

Sure enough, he inherited the captaincy a year later from

Courtney Walsh. But his first stint in charge lurched close to disaster till it was rescued by his own magical batting.

Against the best team in the world, West Indies cricket hit its nadir to be all out for 51 in the first Test at Port of Spain.

The knives were now out for his scalp and he responded in the grandest manner. Against the formidable bowling of McGrath, Gillespie and Warne, he peeled off peerless innings of 213, 100 and 153 not out and the series was drawn 2-2.

It was arguably the brightest moment in the last 10 years for the West Indies, a period of massive lows and occasional highs.

On a personal level the biggest high came in April 2004 when he regained the world Test record, snatched by Mathew Hayden six months earlier with 380. Now Lara's 400 not out against England at St. John's made him the first in Test cricket to record a quadruple hundred and only the second after Bradman to have two scores of 300-plus.

Then, later that year West Indies gave fresh hope to their fans around the world when Lara led them to victory in the Champions Trophy in England.

Though they reached the final of the same event last year in India, any hopes of a revival turned out to be a mirage.

With the dismal performance in the World Cup in front of their own adoring supporters, West Indies cricket continues to be marooned in the desert.

Lara's fascinating journey has come to an end. But whether his retirement leaves a hole in the team or instead leads to a revival is something that we shall all follow with intense interest.

□

(sulekha.com, 20/3/07)

Status Symbol

This was written at a time when Sachin Tendulkar was going through an uncharacteristic slump. He has put that firmly behind him now.

Sachin Tendulkar's fourth and probably final tour of England comes at perhaps the lowest point in his career.

No longer is he the leading icon of Indian cricket—that mantle has passed onto captain Rahul Dravid.

On his first tour in 1990, Tendulkar was the teenage prodigy whose maiden century in the Old Trafford Test saved India's cause and marked him out to be a champion of the future.

Six years later when he returned to England he was by now widely recognised as the world's leading batsman.

By the time of Tendulkar's third visit in 2002, he had achieved senior statesman status in the side and scored his fourth century in 10 Tests on English soil at Leeds.

But over the last five years his moments of glory—top scorer in the 2003 World Cup, holder of the world record for most Test centuries—have been largely overshadowed by a downward spiral of fortunes.

A spate of injuries have taken an increasing toll on the world's most experienced cricketer—he made his debut in 1989 in Pakistan.

Most of those injuries have been a result of the wear-and-tear of international cricket, the most serious of them being a back injury in 1999 and a bout of tennis elbow that stuck him in July 2004 that looked like it would bring his career to a premature close.

Others have been suffered on-field. But the end result has been a startling decline in form since 2002 with the lean batting patches getting longer and longer.

'Cricket is our religion, Sachin is our god' was a popular banner seen around the world wherever Indian cricket fans turned up to support their team.

No longer. After a miserable World Cup in the West Indies, the final taboo in Indian cricket had been breached—there were calls for Tendulkar to be dropped.

Indeed, technically he was for the tour of Bangladesh in May though the selectors chose to go with the 'rested' euphemism after he was excluded for the ODI series.

Considering the intense public and media scrutiny our cricketers are subjected to, it is something of a miracle that

Tendulkar was able to maintain a glittering public persona for so long. Till things began to go downhill over the seemingly innocuous issue of receiving a car from sponsors Fiat while touring England in 2002.

It was no ordinary car though. Michael Schumacher at Silverstone handed over to Tendulkar the keys to a Ferrari and that would cause the first perceptible dent in his public image.

Tendulkar has a passion for Formula-1 and driving fast cars, even though Mumbai's roads are hardly conducive to such passions.

The tax imposed on luxury foreign cars is considerably higher than the cost of the vehicle itself and after Tendulkar sent a written request to the Government, the charges were waived. Following a public outcry the manufacturers paid the costs on his behalf. But the damage had been done.

His recent broad public hints about a desire to regain the captaincy for the third time have not gone down well either.

The frisson of excitement that surged around cricket grounds of the world at Tendulkar's imminent entry to the crease has dissipated over the last few years.

The drastic transformation from his 'Master Blaster' image—a tag he inherited from his idol Viv Richards by the mid-90s—has come about with his decision to be more the accumulator than the destroyer.

Whether it is the onset of age (he has been on the international cricket circuit for 18 of his 34 years) or the never-ending cycle of injuries, what is certain is that we will only get rare glimpses of the batsman who took apart some of the greatest bowlers of his era, most notably Shane Warne.

Those glimpses are still seen in the shorter version of the game. In Test matches though that exciting era appears to have passed for good, adding to the loss of adulation.

Indian cricket fans over the generations have become accustomed to displays of technical excellence in the manner of Vijay Merchant, Sunil Gavaskar and Dravid or the wristy elegance of GR Viswanath, Mohammad Azharuddin and Sourav Ganguly.

There have been only rare instances in these past 75 years when Indians have witnessed a batsman going after the bowler. The country's first captain CK Nayudu was an early example though he played only seven Tests. Wicket-keeper Farokh Engineer and all-rounder Kapil Dev followed the tradition.

But in Tendulkar India had at last found a batsman who could change the course of a Test match in the matter of one session with his audacious strokeplay.

It was in the fourth and final Test at Sydney in January 2004 that Tendulkar Version 2.0 was unveiled to the public.

His previous five innings in the series had produced scores of 0, 1, 37, 0, 44. Further, in 14 Tests abroad over the last two years, he had scored just two centuries.

Now with the series locked at 1-1, India desperately needed runs from their star batsman.

The result was a monumental innings of 241 not out which stretched to over 10 hours. India after winning the toss batted into the third morning to accumulate 705 for 7 declared. It meant there was too little time to bowl Australia out twice and the golden opportunity of a maiden series win in Australia was squandered.

Earlier this year in Cape Town the series was similarly locked. Just when quick runs were needed, the world's most experienced batsman allowed debutant spinner Paul Harris to get on top of him in the second innings to eke out 14 runs in 88 minutes. The Test and series were lost.

His two centuries in two Tests in Bangladesh in May were his first tons since December 2005. But even against a pop- gun attack on flat tracks, the glittering strokes were missing.

Interestingly, Gavaskar who was an early mentor to Tendulkar, took the exact opposite route. Watching him attack the bowling in the last four years of his career was an eye-opener to those accustomed to the rock-solid opening batsman of the 70s.

Tendulkar has rarely responded verbally to his critics. That changed last year when he lashed out at former teammate Sanjay Manjrekar who in an article accused the champion batsman of suffering from a "fear of failure".

The series in England affords him the best opportunity to bury those doubts once and for all.

□

(England and Wales Cricket Board (ECB) souvenir, June 2007)

Indian Summer

The 2007 tour of England marked the 75th anniversary of India's maiden Test match played at Lord's.

The first cricket sides from India to visit England were the Parsees (the first community to take to cricket) in 1886 and 1888 and the 'All-India' side of 1911.

All three tours were unmitigated disasters.

India made their debut in Test cricket at Lord's on 25 June 1932, losing the match by 158 runs though creating a very favourable impression. But there was plenty of drama and intrigue before, during and after the Test.

Having been granted Test status by the ICC (Imperial Cricket Conference) in 1929, the maiden Test match was to be played on Indian soil in 1930-31. However, England's tour was cancelled when Mahatma Gandhi launched the Civil Disobedience movement in January 1930. The threat of England's matches being boycotted forced the hand of the MCC and plans for the next season were also scrapped on similar grounds. .

New Zealand had joined the Test fraternity in 1926 and the West Indies two years later. With India's entry, the family had expanded to six members.

It would be 20 years before the next inclusion, that of Pakistan which had been created out of the partition of India in 1947.

Indian cricket had first been given an identity on the world stage in the 19th century by the exploits of Prince Ranjitsinhji. He was followed in the 1920s by his nephew Duleepsinhji as well as the Nawab of Pataudi, all royalty studying and living in England.

But when it came time to choose a captain for the first Indian Test team an early suggestion was that of an Englishman born in Bombay, Douglas Jardine. Wiser counsel prevailed and even as India were touring in 1932, Jardine was experimenting with the 'bodyline' tactics he would unleash with such devastating effect in Australia later that winter.

It was a tough baptism all right, but one which Indian cricket emerged from with much honour and credit.

Behind the scenes though honour was in short supply. Late night carousing and drunken bouts were the norm among the tourists, most of who were traveling outside India for the first time.

No 'Fredalo' type incidents have been reported, but CK Nayudu, the senior member of the side came in for much abuse when he tried to rein in the wild lot.

Nayudu was India's first cricket superstar and fittingly he led the side onto the field at Lord's on June 25.

But his ascension to the post was through a torturous and Byzantine path and was a far from happy choice for a particular clique within the touring team who loathed him with a vengeance.

Much of this animosity was due to the fact that by 1932 Nayudu had at the age of 37 acquired iconic status among Indian cricket fans. He also had a military background and was a stickler for discipline.

In fact it was a spectacular innings played by Nayudu at Bombay in 1926 against the first official MCC side to India that did much to convince the ICC that India were ready to be promoted to the big league. That innings has acquired legendary status in the annals of Indian cricket and to this day no Indian batsman has matched it in terms of boundaries, or indeed historical significance.

Led by Arthur Gilligan and including such well known players are Maurice Tate, Andy Sandham and wicket-keeper George Brown, the MCC were in India to test the waters and report back to Lord's.

Bombay's population was just about a million and yet 25,000 packed into the Gymkhana ground to watch Somerset's Guy Earle (130) hammer the Hindu bowlers on the first day for 8 sixes and 11 fours as MCC raced to 363.

The next day though Nayudu outdid Earle and had the crowd in raptures. His amazing innings of 153 in 115 minutes contained a world record 11 sixes and also 13 fours and was made out of 187. The Hindus fell just seven short of MCC's total.

Gilligan was certainly convinced the Indians were up to it and six years later the dream of millions of Indian cricket fans had come true.

Intrigue though was an integral part of Indian cricket in the early years. Much of this was due to the royalty factor. Though India's princes were the early patrons of cricket, they also exacted a heavy price with their petty jealousies and constant bickering.

One of the most generous benefactors was the Maharaja of Patiala and he was chosen as captain. His vice-captain was Prince Ghanshyamshinhji of Limbdi while the incongruous role of 'deputy vice-captain' was granted to the Maharajah of Vizianagaram ('Vizzy'), Patiala's bitter rival.

But both Patiala and 'Vizzy' withdrew from the side though the latter would gain the coveted post for the 1936 tour. He remains perhaps India's most despised cricketer for his quisling ways.

Now the Maharajah of Porbander was appointed captain.

He had no pretensions to being a cricketer though and in his first four matches in England he had scores of 0,2,0,2 and 2.

Scorned by the media as the only cricketer in England to have more Rolls Royces than runs, he withdrew from the rest of the tour ostensibly on health grounds.

His brother-in-law Limbdi took over as captain. A somewhat better batsman, he had to withdraw from the Lord's Test due to an injury. And so the mantle fittingly fell on Nayudu.

But India's cricketers who would be feted as heroes on their return home, came perilously close to boycotting the one-off Test. They were used to being led by royalty but could not stomach a fellow-commoner being captain. Late at night they made their stand clear to Porbander and it was only at 4 a.m.—just hours before the Test was to begin—that the air was cleared.

Speculation was rife that India would be routed. Just 10 days earlier Percy Holmes and Herbert Sutcliffe had recorded their world record opening stand of 555 for Yorkshire against Essex. What chance did India's bowlers have?

It's difficult to tell then who was more surprised after the first hour's play with England reeling at 19 for 3, England's cricketers and the spectators or the Indians!

Mohammed Nissar bowled both the openers in his second over and Frank Woolley was run out spectacularly by Lall Singh.

England struggled to 259 all out, Nissar picking up five wickets. But with the English bowlers making up for the lapses of their batsmen, India were bowled out for 189. Nayudu was top scorer with 40.

England declared their second innings at 275 for 8 and this time India could muster only 187. But so impressed was Neville Cardus that he made an appeal to allot the Indians an extra Test.

Back home there was great joy that the players had acquitted themselves so creditably. The cracks within were papered over.

The playing XI at Lord's was a perfect mix between the myriad communities of India—four Hindus, four Muslims, two Parsees and a Sikh. All four Muslims moved to Pakistan in 1947.

Jahangir Khan, the last of the famous side to pass away in 1988, saw his son Majid and nephews Imran Khan and Javed Burki captain Pakistan.

Nayudu continued playing first-class cricket astonishingly till the age of 68—he was to die four years later in 1967.

Seventy-five years later after the first Test, it is Rahul Dravid who proudly carries on the Nayudu tradition.

□

(England and Wales Cricket Board souvenir, June 2007)

Obnoxious Breed?

The Indian tour of Australia in 2007-08 was one of the bitterest in cricket history. Its repercussions are still being felt.

Douglas Jardine, John Snow, Mike Brearley, Richard Hadlee, Muthiah Muralitharan, Sourav Ganguly, Andre Nel…and now Harbhajan Singh.

What do these cricketers have in common? Simple—they have all been vilified as 'hate figures' while touring Australia.

Australia is the most successful cricketing nation in the history of the game, whether it be Test, ODIs or women's cricket. Their cricketers like to portray themselves as playing the game "hard but fair" though that tag is beginning to wear thin.

The Aussie crowds—though fiercely loyal to their own— have also acknowledged champion players from opposing sides. Sachin Tendulkar, Colin Cowdrey, Frank Worrell, Garry Sobers and Vivian Richards amongst others have been great favourites Down Under despite dominating Australian teams over the decades.

Yet lurking in the shadows of Australian cricket has been this history of vilifying opponents who have got under their skin, sometimes with good reason (Jardine) and sometimes for no discernible reason (Hadlee) other than anger and resentment at watching their beloved green and gold warriors being knocked over.

It is somewhat futile but tempting all the same to pigeon-hole these hate figures in one neat category.

Single-minded, to the point of cussedness? Perhaps. Controversial? For the most part. Successful against Australia? Certainly, though by varying degrees.

A major factor in whipping up the frenzy against Harbhajan on this tour was the media, often referred to as the 12th man of the Australian cricket team.

With a few exceptions such as Mike Coward and Peter Roebuck, Australian cricket journalists are remarkably jingoistic in support of the national side.

Not that the Indian media, both traveling with the team and at home, exactly covered themselves with glory. But at least this time they could have been excused considering the provocation from their Aussie counterparts.

It has long been understood that the media would mount a concerted attack on the star player of the visiting teams, most often the captain.

Jardine, Brearley and Ganguly all fall into this category though in the case of Jardine his Bodyline tactics aimed principally at Australia's darling Don Bradman was enough to turn the crowds against him. The media did not really have to play a very active role in the case of the reviled England captain on that fiery 1932-33 tour.

Seventy-five years later there has been a sea-change as Harbhajan will attest to. And much of it is due to the all-pervasive nature of the electronic media with TV and still cameras all around the ground capturing every moment of every game and the Internet becoming a filter-free outlet for often vile and racist rants.

Australian crowds like their media also have a poor reputation. This is largely due to the large intake of beer that turns the crowd violent and unruly.

Racism is never far from the surface and though the barracking of Muralitharan was essentially due to his controversial bowling action, there was always something more sinister about the attacks.

The last straw for the Sri Lankan world record holder came in 2004 when John Howard, then the Australian Prime Minister publicly condemned him, leading Murali to pull out from touring Australia and vowing never to return, though he went back on that.

The chants of 'no-ball' each time he came on to bowl though pale in comparison to the hostility faced by Richard Hadlee, New Zealand's champion bowler who tormented the cream of Australia's batting throughout the '80s.

'Hadlee is a wanker' was the cry, plastered too on posters and banners around the grounds.

Hadlee has recounted in his autobiography how he was the target of abuse from kids as young as five or six, "no doubt egged on by their parents."

The Australian captain of the time, Greg Chappell told Hadlee to treat it as a compliment as the fans realised he was a threat to their side. But he rejected that contention.

"I will always maintain Australian crowds," Hadlee wrote in his 1989 autobiography *Rhythm and Swing,* " as a rare sporting (or unsporting) breed, are the most unruly in the world."

Jardine's opinion of Australians was even less complimentary. The mutual animosity began on his first tour in 1928-29 when he was new to the team and then blew up when he returned as captain four years later. He usually referred to them as uneducated bastards!

Sydney-based cricket author Kersi-Meher Homji sums things up: "For boozed up Oz spectators, it is 'If you can't beat them, boo them.'"

□

(DNA—Daily News and Analysis, 6/3/08)

Hockey, The Crying Game

Being an Indian sports fan—not just a journalist—has been a roller-coaster ride. This was one of the lowest points.

In 40 years of passionately following sports, nearly 30 of which have been spent as a journalist, there are just two occasions on which I can recall shedding tears of disappointment.

While cricket has been my abiding passion since childhood, it is hockey that has an emotional hold on me. I believe that is the case with many of my fellow-countrymen.

It is impossible to decide which is our national sport. But it is hockey that brought us glory on the world stage even before India made its bow in international cricket in 1932. And remember, hockey is played by more than 100 countries around the world.

It was in 1973 when India lost the World Cup final to the hosts the Netherlands—that too after leading 2-0 at half-time—that the tears of anger, frustration and bitterness began to flow.

Then at Sydney in 2000 with qualification for the Olympics semifinals just a whisker away, India botched it in their final league match against Poland. They needed to win or even draw 2-2. The match ended 1-1.

As a professional on the job on a wet and dark evening, I guess I had no business to show my emotions. But I was not the only one in the press box at that miserable moment to let it all out.

While tennis and cricket were my father's favourite sports,

hockey was my mother's reason to play hooky from college. Especially if she had the chance to watch her heartthrob, the dashing AIS Dara (who would move to Pakistan after Partition).

Till one day she was caught out—the next day's newspaper had her photo cheering from the crowd!

With cricket being held the year round and set to increase even more now with the various 20/20 *tamashas,* it's hard to place a memorable event into perspectives of time and place.

What really counts in hockey are the Olympics and the World Cup with the Asian Games a distant third. And in all these events it is still an India-Pakistan tie that sets the pulses racing.

It was probably the first time in nearly 200 years of existence at our school in Calcutta that morning assembly was temporarily put on hold. Even the teachers were beside themselves with excitement as Aslam Sher Khan saved India's skin in the semifinals of the 1975 World Cup. And then came the triumph in the final against Pakistan. Oh joy of joys! Sadly, there was no live TV to watch our heroes in their moment of glory.

Twenty years later I asked Aslam to sign my schoolboy scrapbook of photos and cuttings of that memorable event. "*Purane yaadein*" (old memories) he said as his eyes welled up.

Indian hockey's golden chance came at the final of the 1982 Asian Games in New Delhi. With the who's who of the Capital out in force, India struck first against Pakistan.

Then came the deluge as we were overwhelmed 1-7. It was a humiliation that has now been matched 26 years later.

Cricket on the other grabbed its chance. Just a year after the Asian Games our boys stunned themselves as much as the cricket world by winning the Prudential World Cup in England. And ever since then it has been a one-horse sporting race in India.

In faraway Chile the last nail was hammered into Indian hockey's coffin last week. What a long journey it has been from Amsterdam in 1928 to Santiago in 2008.

□

(Hindustan Times, 19/3/08)

The Money Game

I have been an IPL cynic from the start. This was the first of my critical pieces. The ICL and Stanford are history and the IPL is now under the scanner.

The French have a phrase 'plus ca change...' which roughly translated means 'the more things change, the more they remain the same.'

The French are not big cricket buffs, but the phrase keeps cropping up in my mind whenever cricket hits a new crisis or controversy.

Controversy there has been plenty already. But crisis?

To explain, one must go back over 250 years to the very beginnings of organised cricket.

Coloured clothing? The first professional teams riding horseback and by stagecoach through the length and breadth of England from the mid-18th to early 19th centuries wore coloured shirts to help identify their clubs.

Those professionals would receive challenges from clubs and villages around England and would be paid handsomely for their skills. There were thus plenty of historical precursors to Kerry Packer and his traveling circus of pros including William Clarke (of the 1840s) and Thomas Lord (the founder of Lord's cricket ground) a century earlier.

The first recorded match in which prize money (10 Pounds

Sterling) was on offer was played in 1700. Just 50 years later the first and most famous professional cricket club was formed at Hambledon, Hampshire (referred to as 'the cradle of cricket').

By the 1830s the railways were opening up new avenues and trains began to replace the horseback pro, leading to the wider spread of cricket.

Bookies and match-fixing? You better believe it. Cricket faced its first major crisis when the cover was blown on these professional cricketers indulging in widespread betting and fixing as well as violence and rampant alcoholism.

This was when the amateurs emerging from the elite schools of England such as Eton and Harrow and colleges like Oxford and Cambridge took control of the game and began establishing the county championship in the 1850s, though 1873 is generally regarded as the first year of the championship. This brought to an end the era of the traveling professional circus.

The Marleybone Cricket Club (MCC) was established as the guardian of the game and it's rules and spirit with Lord's as its headquarters.

The division between amateurs (known as 'gentlemen') and professionals (aka 'players') remained in English cricket till it was formally abolished after the 1963 season.

There are uncanny resemblances between those horseback professionals of 250-plus years ago and the modern day cricketer. And a conflict is brewing as more and more super-rich businessmen with giant egos and fortunes to match crop up to up the ante and attract the top players to their fold.

Thus more than a century after the establishment of the county championship in England spelled the end of the traveling professional, history is about to be neatly reversed.

The first of these cricket-oriented businessmen in the modern era was of course Packer and his two-year World Series Cricket that was launched in Australia in the 1977-78 season (and wound up a season later) and was the biggest force for change in cricket in the 20th century.

Since then the late Packer has had clones springing up all over the cricket world.

Sheikh Abdul Rahman Bukhatir was the first to follow in Packer's footsteps. He launched cricket in the Sharjah desert with exhibition matches between India and Pakistan in 1981.

Two years later, having learned an expensive lesson at the hands of the Australian media tycoon who sued and won, the respective national bodies decided to co-operate with Bukhatir and his right-hand man, former Pakistan captain Asif Iqbal and the Cricketers' Benefit Fund Series (CBFS) was born.

The matches received official sanction and the tournaments were a huge success whenever India and Pakistan faced off.

But the emergence of the crime underworld attracted the attention of the Indian government and once the Indian board withdrew their team in 2000, the curtains came down on the show.

There is now the spectre of the betting mafia once again descending on world cricket. 20/20 cricket is an ideal format for illegal betting (and its evil off-shoot, match-fixing) and herein lies the danger of this new format and its many avatars.

The IPL was launched by the BCCI to counter the Indian Cricket League (ICL), the brainchild of Essel chairman Subhash Chandra who like Packer 30 years earlier was thwarted in his bid to get the exclusive cricket telecast rights for his own Zee TV network.

The sporting world was stunned by the auction of nearly 80 international cricketers in Mumbai with the fat cats of Indian business combining with Bollywood's glamour boys and girls. The eight franchise teams floated by the IPL had earlier attracted massive price tags and now it was the cricketers who for the first time found themselves on the auction block.

It was India's ODI and 20/20 captain MS Dhoni who attracted the biggest price tag of $1.5 million followed closely by Australian all-rounder Andrew Symonds.

But just as Bukhatir offered more riches than Packer and the

IPL has gone one up on the ICL in the financial stakes, now comes the news that the IPL too is being put in the shade by Texas oil billionaire Sir Allen Stanford.

Stanford has made Antigua his home and has completed a stunningly successful second year of his Stanford 20/20 tournament involving 20 island nations of the Caribbean (Cuba will join next year), all playing at his own Stanford cricket ground in Antigua. This is the home of Sir Viv Richards who heads his 'legends' band of consultants made up of the greatest living cricketers from the West Indies.

Initially opposed to this private cricket event, the West Indies Cricket Board had no option but to dance to Stanford's tune considering they are one of the most impoverished cricket boards in the world.

In 2006 Stanford offered $5 million for a one-off match between South Africa and his West Indies 'All Stars', the cream of the crop chosen from his own tournament. That never came off due to official opposition from both boards.

Last year after India won the inaugural T-20 World Cup in South Africa, Stanford upped the stakes, this time putting up $10 million for a match between the world champs and the West Indies.

The response? "They [the BCCI] said, 'no, we don't want to do that because it would be endorsing a privately funded programme,'" according to Stanford. "And look what they've done. They've set up their own privately funded programme. This is all about business, and its big time business."

He calls those who have signed up with the IPL as "mercenaries" which is a bit hard to swallow.

Clearly miffed, Stanford has now doubled the prize money and Australia have been invited. "$20 million for 20/20 cricket" he is calling it and who can resist? Certainly not the cricketers.

Yes, believe it or not, a winner-takes-it-all one-off match between the West Indies and Australia for $20 million!

Suddenly Dhoni's price tag for the one IPL season is beginning to look like peanuts. Imagine being in a position to earn that kind of money for a game lasting barely three hours.

So what is to stop some other billionaire from some other part of the world doubling that amount? Say for argument's sake, the Sultan of Brunei who has a passion for cricket and once employed Sir Viv to personally coach his son?

"Maybe another millionaire will come in with a different competition. Hopefully, it won't be too long," West Indies star batsman Chris Gayle (IPL price tag $800,000) was quoted after his side Jamaica lost in the final of the Stanford 20/20 to Trinidad.

So instead of riding on horseback to play in challenge matches around England as professional cricketers did 250 years ago, we may soon witness the spectacle of the modern-day pro flying around the globe from one private league to another to line his pockets.

The ICC will be just a mute spectator and probably killed off, as banning players will only bring in the restraint of trade law as Packer's men did successfully 30 years ago.

It was respected Australian cricket author and journalist Gideon Haigh who wrote a few years back that it was the winner-takes-it-all concept of prize money first introduced in the modern era (it was the same in the 18th and 19th century) by Packer that laid the seeds for match-fixing in the last years of the 20th century.

If some of the captains of that time could sell their national pride for financial gain from illegal bookies, can one expect today's cricketers to feel even a shred of loyalty while playing 20/20 matches, that too for franchises?

Further, the ICC has deemed the IPL a domestic event and will not be deploying its Anti-Corruption Unit (nor its drug-testing labs) at either the IPL or at Stanford's events. And the 'rebel' ICL is beyond their purview.

Already the ICC and the Federation of International Cricketers' Association (FICA) have expressed grave concerns over the threat of match-fixing in these new leagues.

The conflict with the traditional Test and ODI calendar is

already obvious while a spate of international cricketers have been announcing their retirements in order to concentrate on these lucrative leagues. National bodies around the cricket world are running for cover, unable to stanch the outflow of their players.

20/20 cricket it appears has opened a Pandora's Box.

□

(Sportstar Weekly, 19/4/08)

Long Term Implications of IPL Ominous

This was written during the first season of the IPL. Despite its financial success, I could not conceal my fears and had a foreboding of what was to come.

The apparently resounding success of the Indian Premier League, barely past the halfway mark of its first season has seen the already loose rules and regulations being twisted and turned to suit the franchise owners who are calling the shots.

The tournament was launched in a knee-jerk manner in order to crush the breakaway Indian Cricket League at its nascent stage.

It may have succeeded in doing just that. But the long-term implications of the IPL taking off so early with the paying public are ominous for the future of world and Indian cricket.

How so? Just study the signals being given off by IPL commissioner Lalit Modi.

The salary cap per team of $5 million imposed on the franchises for the first season was hotly contested by the owners. Now they have got their way and Modi has been boasting to the foreign media how cricketers next season could end up being the highest-paid sportsmen in the world.

While Dhoni landed the largest contact this season of $1.5 million, Australia's cricketers are reporting this could zoom up to

$15 million next year.

The resulting explosion in salaries means the vast majority of international cricketers will simply walk away from their national teams.

It is already happening with the sudden retirements of a spate of players and polls of Australian and English cricketers have revealed alarming results—the IPL (and ICL, while it lasts) is now the priority for a significant number.

Even this season with the salary cap in place, there were murmurs of protest among the Australian, West Indian and New Zealand players who had to leave the IPL early on for national duty. No doubt some of them would have been happier not to get selected for their country so that they could stay on and make hay in the IPL.

The temptation will be even greater for both players and coaches to ditch their nations once the cap goes. Already New Zealand coach John Bracewell has indicated he will soon step down with an eye on the IPL.

And India's grassroots cricket structure is rapidly falling apart. Which child will nurture dreams any more of playing for India when he can get a packet parading his skills in the IPL?

Modi's loud noises of a player requiring an NOC (No Objection Certificate) from his national association in order to play in the IPL will be quickly forgotten next year, mark my words. The result will be a total disintegration of the world cricket structure as we know it.

The farce surrounding banned Pakistan fast bowler Shoaib Akhtar's sudden appearance in the IPL despite his ban is a sign of things to come. It is pretty obvious that the BCCI/IPL authorities with all their financial clout, put pressure on the PCB (Pakistan Cricket Board) to release him this season.

National cricket associations around the world and the ICC as well will stand helpless before the money power of the IPL if it becomes successful and a time will come when the number of franchise teams will start growing from the current eight.

In that probable scenario, the six-week window which the IPL is asking/demanding from the ICC will also grow till the international cricket calendar set by the ICC will cease to exist or even matter.

Now we are being informed via Shane Warne that the cap of four foreign players in the playing XI of each franchise is also likely to be lifted next season.

All this pious talk of the IPL being beneficial to young Indian cricketers will therefore go up in smoke, once again on the demand of the franchise owners.

There has also been the farcical situation in the IPL where umpires' and Match Referees' actions are being called into question. So who will police the police?

That is not all. A Chennai newspaper has questioned the credibility of the drug testing procedures of the IPL. This is a serious issue that needs explaining by their head honchos.

The biggest danger to the league though is the spectre of match fixing. And it is a daily from New Delhi that has exposed the presence of a top Delhi and District Cricket Association (DDCA) official sitting in the Delhi Daredevils dressing room during Thursday's match at the Kotla, busy talking on his cell phone. The man in question is a well known bookie in the Capital.

The ICC made it clear that the IPL is a domestic tournament and their Anti-Corruption and Security Unit (ACSU) officers would not be present.

Team dressing rooms are a no-go area during international matches for all but players and support staff such as coaches and physios.

The dressing room during the IPL tournament is no longer off limits though with franchise owners, their staffers and assorted hangers-on enjoying open access, much to the consternation of the players.

It is also rapidly beginning to sink in for them that being owned by someone rich and powerful can be a humiliating business if things don't click.

The IPL is fast becoming a law unto itself, its backers drunk on power, money and fame.

A leading national daily has exposed the nexus between the top brass of the IPL and the BCCI and various IPL franchises.

When the commissioner of the IPL has been revealed to have family links with two of the teams and two top BCCI officials have team connections as well, is it not obvious now that the whole exercise has become a vehicle for the personal aggrandisement of a favoured few at the expense of cricket as we have known and loved it for over a century?

□

(rediff.com, 12/5/08)

Beginning A New Chapter

Cricket and the Olympics have been my greatest sporting passions. Reporting on the 2000 Sydney Olympics was the highlight of my career.

Sport, we are told mirrors society. The Summer Olympics which is staged every four years (as is the Winter Olympics) and is the showpiece for the planet's sporting talent is a testament to this saying. Little has changed in this regard for over 2,500 years.

The Olympics were revived in the modern era after a gap of over a millennium thanks largely to the missionary zeal of Frenchman Baron Pierre De Coubertin.

The first modern Olympics were fittingly staged at Athens—birthplace of the ancient Games—in 1896.

Logically and historically, the centenary of the Modern Olympics should have been held at Athens too in 1996.

Greece lobbied to stage those special Games as they felt it was their birthright. But they were beaten in the fierce bidding war by Atlanta, USA in what became derisively known as 'The Coca-Cola Olympics.' Atlanta was perhaps the most tawdry of all the modern Olympics.

The Greeks were furious and when their turn finally came in 2004, they put on a grand spectacle. The Olympics had finally returned to their spiritual birthplace.

So competitive has been the bidding by numerous nations to host the Olympics in recent years that the International Olympic Committee (IOC) had to put in place tight regulations after it was rocked by bribery scandals.

A far cry indeed from the early years when the nascent Olympics movement almost died out within a decade of its revival.

Again, in the 1970s the movement faced another crisis when the massive budgets involved forced governments to shy away.

Los Angeles were the sole bidders for the 1984 Olympics and they revived the movement by relying on private funding, television rights sales and corporate funding rather than squeezing the taxpayer as had been the case most notably in Montreal in 1976.

The successive mass boycotts of 1976, 1980 (Moscow) and 1984—as well as the tragedy of Munich (1972)—placed a dark cloud over the Olympics.

Other scandals would follow most notably Ben Johnson's disqualification for doping at Seoul (1988). But today the Olympics are in robust shape as they head into Beijing.

A major reason for this is the lifting on the ban on professional sportspersons which was an integral part of the Olympics charter till professional footballers were allowed to compete in 1984 with the proviso that they had not taken part in the World Cup.

By 1988 the floodgates were opened when professional tennis players were welcomed and by 1992 America's top NBA (National Basketball Association) stars brought glitz and glamour to the Olympics with their 'Dream Teams'. Thankfully today the hypocrisy of 'shamateurism' (professionals posing as amateurs) is a thing of the past.

So too is the Cold War between the West (led by the United States) and the East (led by the former Soviet Union and its Eastern European allies) which died out with the demise of the USSR in 1991 and the fall of the Berlin Wall.

Those Cold War duels did bring an extra competitive edge to international sporting encounters. But they also led to wholesale state-sponsored doping programmes, particularly in East Germany which tainted the Olympics forever.

Doping continues to be perhaps the greatest menace facing world sports today. But at least we will be spared the horrifying sight of Soviet shot putter and discus champion Tamara Press who disappeared once gender tests (since abolished) were introduced in 1968; or the colossal Amazonian East German swimmers of 1976 who terrified their opponents with their steroid-boosted size and strength.

Sporting victories back then were held up as a symbol of the success of the Communist system and no expense was spared in training and funding of sports.

The Chinese still rely on this system, but jingoism in the Olympics—like so much else in this day and age—was prominent during ancient times as well.

Beginning around 776 BC, the ancient Olympic Games were held every four years in the valley of Olympia in Greece.

As their popularity spread, competitors came from not just Greece but from the Macedonian and Roman empires as well.

The Games were treated as a ritual festival and the idea of winning was much more significant in ancient times than in the noble Olympic ideal as established by de Coubertin more than 2,500 years later.

In fact for the Greeks, victory was of paramount importance with defeat bringing disgrace to the whole *polis* (city-state).

Even thousands of years back, though ostensibly the only prize for the winners was an olive wreath placed upon their heads, sportspersons were fully supported during training and handsomely rewarded on winning by their home towns.

The growing popularity of the Games and the rewards that came with winning sure enough brought in cheating, bribery and boycotts, all commonly believed to be modern scourges.

Though women were initially barred, they were finally accepted in 396 BC, nearly four centuries after the start.

By contrast in the modern version, women made their bow in the second edition at Paris in 1900 after being excluded from Athens in 1896. Today their numbers nearly match that of men.

After lasting for more than 1,100 years, the Olympics were abolished in 393 AD by Emperor Theodosius of Rome who considered them pagan.

It would be another 1,500 years before the movement was revived.

The shadow of politics has been a constant at the Olympics right from ancient times and again from 1896 onwards.

Whoever said sport should be free of politics is living in a cocoon. It never has been possible and probably never will be, and this is especially the case at the Olympics which have always been the focus of the world media.

If the Chinese government is facing flak for using the Beijing Olympics to present to the world their picture of a modern, progressive nation it is hardly alone.

In 1896 and again at the 1906 'intercalated' (considered unofficial) Olympics at Athens, the Greek royal family made sure they were always in the spotlight.

The British royal family did the same in London in 1908 as did the Swedes at Stockholm in 1912 where the prizes were handed out by both King Gustav of Sweden and Czar Nicholas of Russia.

Undoubtedly the most pernicious display was perpetrated by Nazi dictator Adolf Hitler at the Berlin Olympics of 1936.

The IOC had awarded Berlin the right to stage the Games in 1931, two years before Hitler seized power in Germany.

He realized the propaganda value of using the event to showcase his racist message of Aryan superiority and no expense was saved to make Berlin'36 a grand success and spectacle.

Debate raged in many nations, notably the United States over whether the Games should be boycotted in protest at the Nazi policy of discrimination against its Jewish population.

In the end, all talk fizzled out. Hitler had his propaganda tool, but thanks to the brilliant efforts of Jesse Owens and other African-American stars, the Nazi myths turned to dust.

The Germans were determined to wipe away those unpleasant memories when the Olympics returned in 1972.

Sadly, Munich will forever be associated with the massacre of Israeli sportsmen at the hands of the PLO death squad and the free, open and friendly spirit of the Games too died a tragic death on German soil. Security today is the number one priority of any organizing nation.

It took a long time, but after the 1960 Rome Olympics, South Africa were banished from the movement for the evil practice of apartheid, or racial discrimination.

They returned at Barcelona in 1992 once majority Black rule was brought in and after the release of Nelson Mandela.

Indeed, the period between Seoul (1988) and Barcelona was one of the most tumultuous in world history and this was reflected at the Olympics. For the first time in 20 years at Barcelona, all nations were represented.

South Africa were back, North and South Yemen were united as were West and East Germany with the fall of the Wall, the Soviet Union split into 15 separate nations and Yugoslavia was beginning to disintegrate.

But the question that was posed some years back by famed Olympic historian David Wallechinsky continues to haunt me.

In Wallechinsky's reasoning, if South Africa could be barred for disenfranchising its non-white population, should not the same action be taken against Saudi Arabia and other Gulf states who continue to exclude more than half their population from participation in sports, or indeed in the case of the Saudis, even from driving?

Countries with men-only Olympic teams apart from Saudi Arabia, include Qatar, the United Arab Emirates and Oman. Iran allows women only to take part in shooting. According to their respective governments, women are barred from Olympic participation for ''cultural and religious reasons."

But time may be running out for them. Pressure has been building for some years and the IOC has indicated nations practicing such discrimination may be barred from the 2012 London Olympics. It would be about time.

If despite all the politics, commercialisation and cheating, the Olympics still stand for something, it is for the full, free and fair participation of sportspersons, irrespective of their religious or political beliefs, gender, sexual orientation or skin colour.

Anything that falls short of these ideals should be considered abhorrent and unacceptable.

□

(India Today Olympics special, August 2008)

The Indian Kaleidoscope

The story of India at the Olympics has been one of miserable failure. This was written prior to Beijing 2008 where things finally looked up.

It was during the 1972 Munich Olympics that International Olympics Committee president Avery Brundage—an Olympic pentathlete and decathlete in his youth—asked a group of Indian journalists what is pertinent even today.

"You are a country of 550 million. Can you tell me why you can't produce a single track and field medalist?"

Even as Bhalindra Singh (president of the Indian Olympic Association) looked around the room nervously, a journalist came to his rescue.

"Maybe because we believe that the important thing is to take part and not to win medals," came the answer, echoing the noble words of Baron Pierre de Coubertin, the founder of the modern Olympics movement.

Now 36 years later, nothing has changed—except the Indian population has doubled to over one billion. And still no track and field medal in sight.

This time at Beijing Indian followers of the Olympics will also have to reconcile themselves to the absence of the hockey team, the one sport that has brought consistent gold medal glory to the Olympic movement in India.

Truth to tell though, even if they had qualified the hockey team would not have been in medal contention.

The last time India won a genuine hockey gold medal was at the 1964 Tokyo Olympics.

In 1968 and 1972, that medal changed to bronze. And though V. Bhaskaran led the nation to gold at the 1980 Moscow Games, it was severely devalued due to the boycott by the major western nations and Pakistan. As it is India just about managed to edge out Spain in the final.

Since then? Not even a semifinal place from 1984 to 2004, though the team came agonizingly close in 1984 and 2000.

To think, India went through three Olympics (1984, 1988 and 1992) without a single medal. It is men's tennis, women's weightlifting and men's shooting that saved us from total ignominy in 1996 (Atlanta), 2000 (Sydney) and 2004 (Athens).

Track and field (athletics)? It looks as if we are no-hopers once again unless long jumper Anju Bobby George can pull off a surprise.

The fourth-place finish for Milkha Singh in the 1960 Rome Olympics (400 metres) and for PT Usha in the 1984 Los Angeles Games (women's 400 metres hurdles), plus a pitiful handful of others who made it to the final of their events, is all we can look back at. A sad situation indeed as India's official participation at the Olympics enters its 80th year at Beijing.

It was at Amsterdam in 1928 that the Indian Olympic Association—under British rule of course—sent a contingent to the Olympics for the first time. The IOA had been officially formed in 1927, though India's National Olympic Committee was registered during the 1924 Paris Olympics.

But India's Olympics participation actually began in 1920 when Bombay industrialist Sir Dorabji Tata sponsored three athletes and three wrestlers. He did the same in 1924 when eight athletes were sent.

In 1927 Tata briefly became the first president of the IOA

before being replaced in the same year by Bhupendra Singh, the Maharaja of Patiala (father of Bhalindra and grandfather of Randhir Singh, the current secretary-general).

It was at Amsterdam too that the magic spell of hockey domination began and continued unabated till India lost to Pakistan in the final at Rome in 1960.

That made it six gold medals in a row plus two more in 1964 and 1980, one silver and two bronze as well.

Legendary names like Dhyan Chand ('The Wizard'), Balbir Singh Dosanjh and Leslie Claudius earned themselves golden hat-tricks. But all that now seems part of ancient history, given the woeful decline of hockey in India.

For the record, the 1920 contingent consisted of (Athletics): Purma C. Bannerjee (100 & 200 metres); Phadeppa F. Chaugle (10,000 metres & Marathon); Sadashjir V. Datar (Marathon). Freestyle wrestling: Kumar Navale (middleweight); D. Randhir Shinde (featherweight) and Jit Singh (featherweight).

One mysterious figure however continues to haunt Indian Olympic fans and historians alike.

Norman Gilbert Pritchard competed in the second modern Olympics at Paris in 1900 and returned with silver medals in the 200 metres and 200 metres hurdles. He also finished fifth in the 110 metres hurdles, but failed to make it to the finals of the 60 and 100 metres.

Born in Calcutta in 1875 of English parents, he studied in St. Xavier's, was the first man to score a hat-trick in Indian football, was secretary of the Indian Football Association (1900-02) and a fixture on the Calcutta sporting, business and social scene till he moved to England in 1904 to trade on the jute market.

He first visited England in 1900 and competed in numerous athletics competitions in London before deciding to cross the Channel and compete in Paris.

Confusion arose as to his nationality as in England he was listed as representing both the Bengal Presidency Athletic Club and the London Athletic Club.

It has to be emphasised here that till 1908 participants entered the Olympics as individuals rather than as selected members of a national team. Indeed the records of the early Olympics are haphazard and have never been given official status by the IOC. The Olympics were so low-key in the early years that many participants were blissfully unaware of its significance.

It has been left to individual historians to decide on contentious issues and the general consensus now is that the medals belong to India, though some in Britain continue to campaign for them.

Pritchard made a name for himself on the stage in Broadway after moving to the United States in 1913. He adopted the name of Norman Trevor and was one of the early stars of the silent movie era in Hollywood in the 1920s.

Sadly he died in penury, a physical and mental wreck in New York in 1929.

Pritchard's legacy died out with him. No Indian athlete since has been able to match his feats.

The saga of Milkha and Usha missing the third place and bronze medal by a whisker is well-known by now. Four other athletes and two women's relay squads have also reached the final of their events, but none looked likely medal prospects.

But there have been other close calls, medals missed under heartbreaking circumstances, all part of the hard-luck story of India at the Olympics.

At the Sydney Olympics light heavyweight (81 kg) boxer Gurcharan Singh was tied on points in his quarterfinal but lost on the cumulative count back system among the five judges. One punch and a couple of seconds more and he could have become India's first boxing medalist.

It was a similar case of heartbreak for bantamweight wrestler Prem Nath who lost the bronze by a mere half point in 1972 and featherweight KD Mangave who was edged out by one point at Helsinki in 1952.

The Indian football side reached the semifinals before losing to Bulgaria in the playoff match for bronze in the 1956 Melbourne Olympics.

At Athens in 2004 former tennis doubles world number one Leander Paes and Mahesh Bhupathi squandered match point after match point in their quarterfinals.

Also at Athens, the women's archery team were edged out 228-227 by France in the quarter-finals.

India won her first official individual medal at Helsinki in 1952 when freestyle wrestler Khashaba Dadasaheb Jadhav claimed the bronze in the 57 kg (bantamweight) category.

Sadly, the story of Jadhav is perhaps the best example of why India cannot ever be a sporting nation. It is a tale of neglect, callousness and tragedy.

There was little funding for sports in India so soon after Independence. It was only the sacrifice of principal Khandekar of Raja Ram College in his village of Karad (Maharashtra) who sold his house that enabled Jadhav to gather the funds to travel to Helsinki.

Apart from the village felicitating their hero on his return, Jadhav got nothing for his feat. A lifetime in the police force ended when he was killed in a road accident in 1988 for which his widow Kusum received Rs. 25,000 as compensation.

It was only in 2001 that he was posthumously awarded the Arjuna Award. No wonder a bitter Kusum expressed her disappointment that her late husband had not received a higher honour for his sterling achievement. The family struggles financially to this day.

That sad story surely sent out all the wrong signals and it would be another 44 years before India eked out another individual medal when tennis star Leander Paes won the bronze at the 1996 Atlanta Olympics.

Helsinki also saw the first Indian woman Olympians. Athletes Nilima Ghose and Mary D'Souza did not break any records, but they were trend setters. Their legacy came to fruition when weightlifter Karnam Malleswari became the first Indian woman to win a medal at the 2000 Sydney Olympics.

Can an Indian at Beijing go one better than shooter Rajyavardhan Singh Rathore, double trap silver medalist at the last Olympics in Athens? Things look bleak. Maybe India needs a miracle of Olympic proportions.

Top 10 Indian Olympians

1. **Dhyan Chand (hockey):** The Wizard, the man who gave India its first global sporting identity, winner of three gold medals (1928-36)
2. **Leslie Claudius (hockey):** Statistically one of the most successful Indian Olympians with three gold (1948,'52, '56) and one silver (1960).
3. **Balbir Singh Dosanjh (hockey**): A golden hat-trick (1948-56) for this goal scorer extraordinaire
4. **Norman G. Pritchard (athletics):** The 'Mystery Man'. Two silver medals in 1900 to which both Great Britain and India stake their claim.
5. **Rajyarvardhan Singh Rathore (shooting):** The first official individual silver medalist for India, in the double trap in 2004.
6. **KD Jadhav (freestyle wrestling):** Independent India's first individual medal winner, the bantamweight bronze at the 1952 Helsinki Games.
7. **Karnam Malleswari (women's weightlifting):** The only Indian woman medalist to date, bronze in the 69 kg category at Sydney 2000.
8. **Leander Paes (tennis):** The doubles specialist who delighted the nation with his bronze medal in singles at Atlanta in 1996.
9. **Milkha Singh (athletics):** Broke the existing Olympic record, but edged out of the medals in the 1960 Rome Olympics 400 metres.

10. **PT Usha (women's athletics):** The first Indian woman to reach a final, fourth in the 400 metres hurdles at the 1984 LA Games.
10. **Neville De Souza (football):** India's hat-trick hero against Australia at Melbourne in 1956. The team finished fourth. □

(India Today Olympics special, August 2008)

Winners United!

Every four years the Olympics presents the world with drama and controversy. Beijing was no different.

Despite some sleights-of-hand and a little nitpicking here and there, China's coming out party at the Beijing Olympics can be deemed a grand success.

The grinding Chinese sports machine had targeted 40 gold medals with the hope of dethroning the United States at the top of the tally at the end of the Games.

They achieved that in grand style, bagging a stupendous 51 gold and a total of exactly 100 medals—the first time an Asian nation has topped the gold medal standings.

The clockwork precision of the hosts—almost scary in its efficiency—in every aspect was enough to give an inferiority complex both to the organizers of the 2012 London Olympics and the large Indian contingent of officials hoping for tips when it comes to staging the Commonwealth Games two years from now.

It is a measure of the success of the unrelenting multi-billion dollar Chinese government system that it was the failures as much as the successes that grabbed the headlines. But more on that later.

If China was the winner in the nation stakes, the images of swimmer Michael Phelps and sprinter Usain Bolt will remain part of the Olympics folklore for eternity.

Both immortalized their names in the pantheon of Olympic

legends, Phelps with his record haul of eight gold medals and Bolt as much with his flamboyance as with his stupendous three world records.

The first week belonged to the American aquaman as he erased the longstanding record of compatriot Mark Spitz and his haul of seven gold medals at Munich in 1972.

Once he exited the pool for the final time at Beijing with seven world records in his kitty, it was time for the Jamaican thunderbolt to take centrestage.

IOC President Jacques Rogge was offended but it appears the rest of the word was enchanted by Bolt's extravagant celebrations.

That chest-thumping, high-stepping exhibition of showmanship a good 15 metres from the finish line may have prevented Bolt from dipping under 9.60 seconds in the 100 metres. But it also had the sporting world enraptured both by his record of 9.69 and the sheer audacity of a man who could be so confident—and a touch arrogant—in the shortest and quickest race at the Olympics.

That he won gold and smashed his own recent world record was jaw-dropping enough. That a few days later he would go onto erase Michael Johnson's 'unbeatable' record in the 200 metres as well left onlookers speechless. Fellow sprinters could only throw their arms up in helpless disbelief.

Back home in the Sherwood Content, Trelawny district of Jamaica his aunt blandly informed the media that Usain's father took the boy to the doctor when he was nine as he was concerned that his son was "mad in the head", such was his manic energy.

Sprinting was the best outlet for all that energy, helped according to his now-doting dad by the nutritious local yam.

The world record in the 4x100 was merely the icing on the cake even as Jamaica—population 2.1 million—dealt a body blow to the United States by clinching both the men's and women's sprints.

Indeed, Beijing marked the lowest point for American track and field since their disastrous showing at Munich 36 years ago.

Every Olympics showcases a tiny nation's achievements.

Remember swimmer Antony Nesty of Suriname and his gold at Seoul 1988?

This time it was Iceland (population 316,250), the Bahamas (330,550) and Estonia (1.34 million) and other tiny nations who found themselves among the medals.

So did India (1.1 billion) with a grand total of three. Just enough for our officials and politicians to excel in their favourite sport of mutual back-patting.

It is another matter that shooter Abhinav Bindra, wrestler Sushil Kumar and boxer Vijender Singh won despite the system and not because of it. But that is another story.

It must have also been daunting to have to deal with the army of TV mikes repeatedly thrust in their faces and asked *ad nauseam:* "how do you feel…?"

The poignant photo of boxer Jitender Kumar's father pleading with TV journalists back home in Bhiwani to be left in peace said it all.

Indian TV viewers though surely deserved a collective gold medal of their own for having to sit through the insufferable *Doordarshan* commentary.

But the big story was China and their stupendous haul of medals. The nation made their bow at a major sporting event at the 1974 Teheran Asian Games but it was not till 10 years later at Los Angeles that they won their first gold at the Olympics.

The Big Red Machine has been unstoppable since and once the government decided to concentrate on multi-sports events for the Beijing Olympics, money was of no consideration. All that mattered was national pride.

If sporting success is the measure of national pride, then China's collective heart must be bursting with joy at the moment. The official expenditure on the fabulous fortnight was a whopping $40 billion, though the majority of that was spent on infrastructure.

But just as the successes were spectacular, so were the failures.

Who could believe the famously inscrutable Chinese could

weep with both joy and despair? Joy there was plenty but despair came when the hero of all China, Athens 2004 hurdler gold medalist Liu Xiang limped out of his heat and plunged a nation into paroxysms of shock, anger and sorrow.

Silver and bronze medalists were made to feel like failures and regularly collapsed in tears. It was enough to make one's heart sink.

China made a clean sweep of their traditional national sport of table tennis, winning every medal on offer and that eased the pain to some extent. Defeat in table tennis would have been unthinkable and sure enough gold, silver and bronze in both men's and women's singles and the two team titles as well were China's with ease.

But it was in the three glamour sports of basketball, track and field and football that they failed to strike gold and that surely will be a sore point for years to come.

Meanwhile, even as China was rolling along relentlessly, Great Britain's zoom up the medals charts stunned themselves as much as the rest of the sporting world.

Funding from the National Lottery which followed a miserable one gold at Atlanta in 1996 appeared to have done the trick. Their haul of 19 gold medals put them above Germany and perennial Commonwealth rivals Australia.

Every Olympics has its heartwarming stories and it was the 10 km Open Water swim race held for the first time that had the most inspiring examples.

Amputee swimmer Natalie Du Toit finished 16th—minus her left leg—moving the winner to announce that the South African deserved a special gold medal for her courage.

The men's winner had his own amazing tale to tell. Dutchman Martin van der Weijden fought back against leukaemia in 2001 and today is the best in the world for all distances up to 25 km.

Thank God for the Olympics. □

(All-Sports Magazine, September 2008)

A Tale of Two Matches

After the shallowness of the first IPL season, the 2008 Chennai Test match against England showed the fans what real cricket was all about.

Watching Sachin Tendulkar and co. effortlessly guide India home against England in the first Test at Chennai on Monday brought back memories of a similar feat 32 years ago.

If in 2008 the victory was achieved with the nation still in shock after the terrorist outrage in Mumbai, in 1976 the Indians chased down a world record target (since beaten) at the Queen's Park Oval in Port of Spain, Trinidad with India under the dark cloud of Emergency rule.

Before the 'SRT Era' of Indian cricket—entering its 20th year next month—there was the 'SMG (Sunil Manohar Gavaskar) Era' stretching back to 1971 when the master opening batsman hit world cricket like a storm in his debut series in the West Indies.

By the time he returned to the Caribbean five years later, West Indies cricket was in the throes of crisis.

Clive Lloyd's team had just returned from Australia where they were smarting under a 5-1 thrashing and the India series was looming as a make-or-break one for the captain.

The home side easily won the first Test at Bridgetown,

Barbados before surviving a close call in the second Test at Port of Spain, Trinidad which ended in a draw.

The third Test to be played at Georgetown, Guyana was a washout and the Indians were back in the Trinidad capital where the third Test match was shifted.

Bishan Bedi and his men were not complaining. In 1971 India had recorded their first win on West Indian soil at the Queen's Park Oval where the wicket traditionally assisted spinners. Besides, the large number of Indian settlers on the island always backed teams from their original homeland. That made the venue like a home-away-from-home for Indian cricket teams. And Gavaskar had a phenomenal record at his favourite ground.

There was little indication that history was in the making over the first four days of the Test as the home side took a big first innings lead of 131 runs and then confidently declared their second innings at 271 for 6 on the fourth afternoon.

In Mumbai too England captain Kevin Pietersen had declared his second innings—though by then England had lost nine wickets—after taking a lead of 75 runs. The target in Mumbai was 387 runs, something that had never been achieved on Indian soil. And to top it all, the final day at Chennai also marked the 75th anniversary of the first Test match played on Indian soil.

The target Lloyd had set India back in 1976 was a massive 403. Only once before in Test cricket had a team scored over 400 to win and that had been achieved by Don Bradman's 'Invincibles' in England in 1948.

Who could have believed the brittle Indian batting could match that feat? Certainly not Lloyd who fatally underestimated the courage and resolve of the Indian batsmen.

Keeping the wicket in mind, West Indies had done the unprecedented by fielding three spinners in their playing XI. But two of them were playing their maiden Test and their lack of experience and nerves were exposed on the final day.

India ended the fourth day at Chennai at 131 for one. At

Port of Spain 32 years earlier, the score stood at 134 for one. Still, in both cases victory on the final day for India seemed improbable.

Unlike in the 'SMG Era' where scoring massive totals in the fourth innings had become something of a habit, Indian teams of the 'SRT Era' have a dismal record in this regard.

With Gavaskar and brother-in-law GR Viswanath both reaching centuries on the final day and Mohinder Amarnath scoring a rock-like 85 (the same as Yuvraj Singh at Chennai), the Indians made it with time to spare.

One of the AIR commentators—no live telecast back then—broke down and wept when the target was reached even as he exclaimed that Mrs. Indira Gandhi's 21 Point Economic Programme had played a part in the victory!

Back home in India, some of the doom and gloom that hung over the nation during the dark days of the Emergency was lifted and there were celebrations across the country.

Hopefully some day, captain Bishan Singh Bedi will finally write his memoirs and we will get to know how he felt in his own words.

The match also changed the course of cricket history. Lloyd had learned his lesson and lost faith in spin. From now West Indian teams would field four fast bowlers and mow down all before them for the next 20 years.

Indeed, in the very next Test at Kingston, Jamaica, the Indian batsmen were subjected to a fearsome bouncer battery which left them battered and bruised. Lloyd kept his job as West Indies won the series 2-1. And for better or for worse, international cricket would never be the same again

Tendulkar's joy and relief at hitting the winning runs at Chennai and the dedication of his century and the victory to those who had lost their lives and fought courageously in Mumbai too brought back the smiles on our faces, albeit briefly.

Both Test matches showcased cricket's healing touch. And

Pietersen's England too deserve our everlasting gratitude for coming back to India and giving a resounding reply to the scourge of terrorism.

□

(The New Indian Express, 17/12/08)

Scary Scenario

It was obvious after the terrorist outrage in Mumbai that the Indian tour to Pakistan in January 2009 could not go ahead. Sri Lanka stepped in to replace India. And then came the attack on their cricketers in Lahore just a couple of months after this article was published.

Public memory sure is short. Hopefully the terrorist outrage in Mumbai won't be forgotten in six weeks or six months or even six years. We owe that much to the victims.

But when opinions are voiced that the Indian cricket team should go ahead with their tour to Pakistan in January 2009 as "terrorists have never targeted sportspersons, it would damage their cause", my first reaction is "forgotten Munich?"

Yes, the Munich massacre of 11 Israeli Olympians (and one West German policeman) at the hands of the Palestine Liberation Organization (PLO) took place in 1972. Thirty-six years may seem an eternity to some. But it really is just a blip on the radar of history.

The Olympics were suspended for 34 hours following the horror. But it was the Israelis who insisted they should not be cancelled and the International Olympic Committee President Avery Brundage's call of "The Games must go on" sent out a resounding message that terror should not and must not be allowed to disrupt our lives.

The English cricket team's decision to return to India for the two Test matches after abandoning the final two ODIs following the Mumbai attacks hopefully sends out the same message.

Certainly Kevin Pietersen and his men will be welcomed back like no previous English team has been to these shores. Hopefully the Indian cricket loving public will respond to the call given by the International Cricket Council and come out in droves to support both the sides. They deserve that much.

Rashid Latif, the permanently disgruntled former Pakistan captain can shout himself hoarse with chants of 'hypocrisy' and 'double standards'. After all, terrorism has reduced Pakistan cricket to an international pariah.

The subtle but vital difference in terror in India from across the border and terror in Pakistan from within their own shores is something probably not worth debating with the likes of Latif. But then Virender Sehwag in his own blunt, rustic manner sums it up best when he quite simply says "India is not Pakistan."

Yes, the mega bucks of Indian cricket and specifically the lucrative 20/20 leagues does play a part in persuading international cricketers to return to India despite terror attacks. Having lost out on the Stanford millions and the IPL in its first season, England's cricketers are desperate to parade their skills in India in order to land juicy contracts for the second season next summer.

Then again, why do you think the Pakistan Cricket Board has welcomed rather than condemned England's return to India? They are on tenterhooks with their financial future hinging on our own decision whether to play there or not and cannot afford to antagonize the mighty BCCI.

The destruction of the iconic Taj Palace hotel in Mumbai was too close for comfort for cricketers around the world and they took it personally. It had been like the lap of luxury for so many of them over the years and their home away from home when in Mumbai. Similar was the case with the Pearl Continental hotel in Rawalpindi which was brought down by terrorists earlier this year and where teams had traditionally stayed.

Cricket teams may have been specific targets in the past too. Just months after the Munich Olympics tragedy, the MCC (England) touring team under the captaincy of Tony Lewis was provided armed security after threats had been received from the PLO.

The New Zealanders had a horrific brush with death in May 2002 in Karachi. Their tour was originally scheduled for that fateful date in history, September 2001 but was pushed back by a few months for obvious reasons.

A bus carrying French submarine engineers was struck by a car bomb right outside the team hotel, killing 11 of those on board.

According to sections of the Pakistan media, it was the cricketers who were the original target. The instructions to the killers was to hit a white mini-bus outside the Pearl Continental hotel which would be carrying foreigners. The Kiwi bus was to leave minutes later. So it could have been a case of mistaken identity which spared them and slaughtered the French instead.

Many of the New Zealanders returned home deeply scarred psychologically and had to undergo counseling to erase the horrific sights that unfolded before them.

The first major cricket boycott almost sabotaged the 1996 Wills World Cup, jointly hosted by India, Pakistan and Sri Lanka even before it had begun.

A car bombing in the heart of Colombo killed scores just days before the start of the event and Australia and the West Indies forfeited their matches rather than travel to the Lankan capital.

A week is a long time in politics, goes the well-known saying. So it is perhaps premature and unrealistic to look ahead to the 2011 World Cup which will be hosted on the sub-continent for the third time and with a fourth host (Bangladesh) for the first time. But fears and doubts are already being voiced.

Another greater and more immediate concern is the 2010 Commonwealth Games in New Delhi. It is one thing to secure a single stadium staging a game of cricket. But to do so for multiple venues and the Games Village across the length and breadth of the sprawling national capital with thousands of participants and officials and lakhs of spectators is a nightmarish thought.

The security budget for the Games which currently stands at Rs. 260 crores (app. $52 million) is likely to soar and there has already been talk of Melbourne as an alternate venue. That would be a serious setback to a nation which harbours ambitions of hosting the Olympics by the year 2020.

Melbourne incidentally budgeted a massive $200 million for security when it staged the Games last in 2006.

The Delhi organizers have vowed after the Mumbai attacks not to turn the city into a "fortress" come 2010. But that was precisely the case when the Capital last staged a multi-sports event, the Asian Games in 1982.

At that time, the terror threat was local. Now it has acquired international dimensions, making the situation even more dangerous.

Speaking to *All Sports* magazine, famed security expert Maroof Raza spelt out the potential threat.

"Terror groups always seek to create chaos and get maximum visibility for their notorious acts. And the Commonwealth Games would be an ideal event for them to attract India's and the world's attention, either just prior to the inauguration or during the opening ceremony. And the terror attacks could come from both those led by an anti-India agenda from across our borders, but also from indigenous groups from within."

When the hotel was attacked in Rawalpindi, it was the last straw for the Champions Trophy which had been slated for Pakistan and which has rapidly turned into the ICC's white elephant. There is a huge question mark now over the future of that tournament.

When the attacks occurred in Mumbai, the 20/20 Champions League and the Indian Cricket League—in addition to the last two ODIs between India and England—were rightly immediately cancelled or put on indefinite hold.

With the international cricket calendar already packed, it will be a huge task to find new dates now for the Champions League. The billion dollar baby may well go the same way as the accursed Champions Trophy.

When bombs killed dozens in Jaipur in May, the foreign players in the Rajasthan Royals team who were holidaying in Goa were ready to take the next flight home.

Shane Warne and Graeme Smith had abandoned tours to the sub-continent before under similar circumstances. But this time in true Godfather fashion, they were given an offer they could not refuse—either stay or kiss goodbye forever to the IPL—by Commissioner Lalit Modi and they promptly came scampering back.

Irony of ironies then that Warne would go onto to lead his no-hopers to the inaugural Indian Premier League title.

It is a fragile and fraught situation indeed when an international sport depends on one country alone to generate up to 75% if its revenue. The financial meltdown is already having an adverse effect on Indian (and world) cricket with the Champions League failing to find a title sponsor.

In the larger realm of things, cricket is of course an irrelevance. But if heaven forbid, India continues to be a target of terror, one of the first victims will be the world of cricket. And much else besides. It is a scary scenario but one which we must be prepared for.

□

(All Sports Magazine, January 2009)

It's Money v National Colour

The club v. country dilemma explored here has emerged as one of the many negative fallouts of the IPL phenomenon.

For over 50 years, the world of football's major headache has been the club v. country struggle.

Cricket has been bedeviled with so many controversies over the last century. But club v. country was one thorny issue it did not have to contend with.

Until now that is. The Indian Premier League in just its second year has plunged international cricketers into a quandary.

Their dilemma is over whether to choose to wear national colours and travel around the world the whole year. Or stick to their IPL franchises and pocket ten times more money for playing six weeks of lightweight cricket in one country.

The issue has come into sharp focus with a number of recent incidents.

The latest of these is the case of England all-rounder Andrew Flintoff of the Chennai Super Kings who with compatriot Kevin Pietersen was the highest bid player this season.

With the prestigious 'Ashes' series later this year in England (as well as the T-20 World Cup), Flintoff's fitness had been a major cause of concern.

He has had to return home after just three games for knee

surgery and will miss next month's Test series against the West Indies. There is a cloud over his fitness for the rest of the international season as well.

Flintoff is part of the England and Wales Cricket Board (ECB) central contracts system. Former England captain Nasser Hussain has attacked the ECB as "wimps" for not insisting the injury-prone Flintoff miss the IPL and rest ahead of the hectic international season.

That is what Cricket Australia did with their fast bowler Shaun Tait. Many top Australians in fact decided to give this IPL season a miss.

Hussain (and Mike Atherton, another former captain) have also attacked English cricketers for being greedy—signing lucrative central contracts and demanding to play in the IPL too.

The top English cricketers held out on signing their central contracts last year when they were refused permission to participate in the IPL inaugural season.

There is also the issue of premature retirements from international cricket. New Zealand's all-rounder Jacob Oram who also plays for Chennai has made it clear where his priorities lie.

While not denying the pride of playing for the country, Oram admits the IPL is all about the money. He says he intends to quit Test cricket in order to preserve his body for the more lucrative and less physically taxing 20/20 leagues springing up around the world.

The latest of these is the just-announced American Premier League to be staged in New York at the end of the year. The APL claims to have signed up a number of recently retired players as well as those connected with the 'rebel' Indian Cricket League.

When Australian media magnate Kerry Packer dropped his World Series Cricket bombshell in 1977, players from around the cricket world (except India) flocked to his 'rebel' league and faced the establishment's wrath.

The difference between WSC and IPL is the latter is part and parcel of the establishment since it comes under the purview of the Board of Control for Cricket in India. In effect and right under the eyes of the hapless International Cricket Council, the BCCI has created a monster which has the money power to change the structure of world cricket as we have known it for nearly 150 years.

On the face of it, the ICC could solve the problem by keeping a window for the IPL when no other international cricket is staged.

However, one can be sure Modi would not be satisfied with just one window. Last year flush with the success of the inaugural season he grandly announced the IPL would have two seasons a year.

Modi and the BCCI may have created a monster but it is far from a Frankenstein's monster which destroyed its creator. Instead it could well be a precursor to multi IPL seasons as well as IPL clones, both sanctioned and unsanctioned (like the APL and ICL) cropping up around the world. In fact Modi has already expressed his wish to take the IPL around the world.

If sponsors, spectators, TV viewers and the players themselves decide city-based franchise cricket is the future, the ICC will cease to exist and so will nation v. nation contests.

There may be no escape from that in our modern market-driven world where the word 'traditionalist' is frowned upon, even despised.

For those of us who have a genuine love for cricket as a sport— as distinct from and opposed to 'show-biz' and 'entertainment'—that is a grim but realistic scenario.

□

(The New Indian Express, 29/4/09)

An Invitation to Anarchy

With the IPL having been unleashed on the cricket world in 2008, the new age of the freelance cricketer had dawned.

History has a funny way of repeating itself when it comes to cricket. For a game that has been played competitively for three centuries, nothing really is new.

Match fixing? It all started in the 18th century when traveling professionals rode on horse-back—and later by train—from village to village, playing for large purses in winner-take-all matches.

Combined with rampant drinking, this invariably led to violence and match fixing and it was in the 1850s that the elite class of England stepped in to cleanse the game and set up the county championship where amateurs ruled over the pros for a century.

The division between amateurs (known as 'gentlemen') and professionals ('players') remained in English cricket till it was formally abolished after the 1962 season.

The first cricketers to be banned for match-fixing? No, not Hansie Cronje, Mohammad Azharuddin and Salim Malik. It was William Lambert. The year? 1817!

Coloured clothing? No, it was not Kerry Packer and his World Series circus of 1977-79 Down Under that was the pioneer. Those same village teams centuries ago would were brightly coloured shirts of red, green, purple, etc. to distinguish which parts of England they were representing.

What about fat-cat businessmen flaunting their wealth and buying up the best players? Long before Kerry Packer, Sir Allen Stanford, Abdul Rahman Bukhatir, Vijay Mallya and Ali Bacher, there was William Clarke (of the 1840s) and other entrepreneurs who would travel the length and breadth of England with their teams of professional cricketers who were paid handsome wages and raked in hefty prize money too.

Plus fat bonuses from shady bookies and punters who had infiltrated the game not long after the first recorded match in which prize money (10 Pounds Sterling) was on offer way back in 1700.

Clarke's story is particularly fascinating. In 1846 he bought up the best cricketers in the land and formed the All England XI under his captaincy, an all-conquering side that took on and invariably trounced challengers throughout England.

But by 1852 champion fast bowler John Wisden—founder-editor of *Wisden Cricketers' Almanack*—broke away with a bunch of young pros who felt Clarke's match fees of 4 to 6 Pounds Sterling per game was insufficient and formed a rival side, the United England XI.

Thus it has forever been with cricket, the so-called 'gentleman's game'. And so it is with England all-rounder Andrew 'Freddie' Flintoff who is being dubbed international cricket's first freelance player.

Flintoff may well be the first of the modern era, though it could be argued that it was Australia's all-rounder Andrew 'Roy' Symonds who had actually beaten Flintoff to that title a few months earlier.

The cases of Flintoff and Symonds are similar though not identical.

Tired of his constant late-night drinking bouts and skirmishes while under the influence of booze, Cricket Australia finally gave Symonds marching orders last year. He has been out of the national team ever since, but that hardly seems to bother him.

In fact, rumours abound that Symonds deliberately broke team rules so he could find a convenient escape clause from national duty.

Symonds' agent had made it clear that now that he did not have national commitments, his client was free to sell his talents to Twenty20 franchises around the world.

At $1.35 million, Symonds was the second highest richest cricketer after MS Dhoni when he was snapped up by the Deccan Chargers in the IPL auctions of last year.

He got to play only four games in the inaugural season in 2008 as he was still a part of the national squad. But this year he was free to play the entire IPL season in South Africa and was one of the stars for the Chargers as they charged from last place to first in the span of 12 months.

Late night boozing sessions don't appear to be an issue with the IPL franchises. Indeed, it is practically a pre-requisite with players' attendance at sponsors' parties a must.

So it is hardly surprising that the Chargers' management have expressed full support for their star player despite his poor disciplinary record.

In the case of Flintoff, he announced his retirement from Test cricket at the end of the recent Ashes series but made himself available for the England squad for 50-over and T-20 Internationals.

But Flintoff's agent has made it clear that he will be available only to play for England if his other professional commitments allow him to. And that is sure to lead to a clash eventually with the ECB and his teammates as well who have already begun to resent his attitude.

Flintoff we are told will be plying his trade—assuming he regains full fitness—in T-20 leagues in India (where he is already signed with the Chennai Super Kings), Australia, South Africa and perhaps in the West Indies as well.

The likes of compatriot Kevin Pietersen, West Indian Chris Gayle—who has already publicly expressed his disdain for Test cricket—and Kiwi Brendon McCullum will be keenly following the Freddie saga. As will be players' agents who are rubbing their hands in glee at the treasures on offer from franchises around the cricket world, far in excess of what they are paid to be on national duty.

The IPL we have been informed will insist on 'No Objection Certificates' from players' home associations. And what if these are withheld? Will we then enter the domain of 'restraint of trade'? For that matter, will the franchise owners not raise a hue and cry if denied the services of their superstars?

So is the concept of freelance cricketers a new one? Not quite. And it was a star Indian cricketer who back in the 1950s caused quite a stir with his demands.

'Vinood' Mankad was considered the world's leading all-rounder when India toured England in 1952. Mankad had an offer from Lancashire League side Haslingden which would pay him over 1,000 Pounds Sterling for the season, a considerable sum of money at the time.

At the peak of his powers, Mankad requested the BCCI to give him an assurance that he would be picked for all four Test matches on the tour so he could turn down Haslingden's offer.

The Board refused. But they were forced to backtrack after the team was humiliated in the first Test at Headingley—scene of the notorious 0 for 4 second innings score-line which continues to mock Indian cricket. Mankad was back for the second Test at Lord's which will forever be dubbed 'Mankad's Match' thanks to his heroic all-round display.

The legendary Garry Sobers too turned himself into a traveling pro in the tradition of the horseback players of the 18th century. He was a big star in English domestic cricket in the 60s and was sensational for South Australia too in the Sheffield Shield.

The difference? He never skipped a Test match for the West Indies in a career spanning two decades. Today's freelance cricketers—and their ever-present agents—appear to have another agenda altogether. And the toothless International Cricket Council can only look on helplessly.

□

(All Sports Magazine, October 2009)

Whose Cricket Team is it?

The questions asked in this article about what the IPL has done for Indian cricket remain unanswered after three seasons of the IPL and yet another abysmal display in an ICC world tournament.

Does the Board of Control for Cricket in India care for Indian cricket? More pertinently, *should* it care for Indian cricket? Not according to its senior counsel and advocate KK Venugopal who five years ago in the Supreme Court made a statement that shocked cricketers and cricket fans throughout the country—'If India plays England, it is a match played by the official team of BCCI and not the official team of India...We do not even fly the national flag nor do we use any national emblem in the activities of the Board."

Rahul Dravid, Sachin Tendulkar, Sourav Ganguly and the rest play for the official team of the BCCI, Venugopal went onto add and not the official team of India.

A group of former 'India' players expressed their sense of outrage and hurt in a joint letter to the BCCI President claiming they had always felt honoured to represent the country and were now distressed by the Board's stand. One is not aware if the Board bothered to respond to them.

The International Cricket Council has recently introduced the playing of the national anthem before each match in their tournaments including the Champions Trophy in South Africa. The sight and sound of foreigners beautifully rendering 'Jana Gana Mana' with the 'Indian' team proudly standing to attention was one of the few highlights of another disappointing tournament for our cricket fans.

Perhaps it is time for the BCCI to inform the ICC that India's national anthem should not be played before their matches and the BCCI could pay a handsome fee to AR Rehman for the use of 'Jai Ho' instead of 'Jana Gana Mana'. Or else the Indian government may be forced to intercede on this matter considering the BCCI's stated legal stand.

The inaugural Champions League to be played between the top 12 Twenty20 teams from around the world (excluding Pakistan, Bangladesh and Zimbabwe) is the latest bogus tournament that the BCCI has cooked up to fill its coffers.

Last month it introduced the Corporate Cup—more or less a 50-over version of the IPL—which had little or no impact on the public and the media.

The BCCI/Indian team's performance in ICC tournaments after 2003—excluding the inaugural World T20 in South Africa in 2007 which it won—has been abysmal. But is the Board really bothered as long as it rakes in the billions and officials, agents, sponsors and select players line their pockets?

IPL czar Lalit Modi had recently said on a TV channel that the IPL had produced "the greatest cricket display in the history of the game."

Yet both team coach Gary Kirsten and captain MS Dhoni have stated that the IPL is nothing but a low-grade domestic tournament and should not be the basis for selection for international cricket.

Here is a question for the BCCI and cricket fans— can you name one Indian cricketer in the last two seasons who has excelled in the IPL and then gone onto make a mark in international cricket? The answer is plain and simple—not a single one. But the coach and captain whose opinion should count and not Modi's have promptly been gagged by the Board. The truth after all invariably hurts.

What the IPL has succeeded in doing is creating a new generation of half-baked players with faulty techniques who strut around like superstars based upon their dubious performances in the IPL.

This year in South Africa Manish Pandey became the first Indian player to score a century in the IPL. He is nowhere in the 'national' reckoning but in a recent interview he glibly explained how he has attained celebrity status due to that century. And proudly stated he now wears tight shirts with buttons open, low-waist jeans and spikes his hair. The poor deluded young man!

Last year after the first IPL season, Dhoni skipped the Test series in Sri Lanka that immediately followed, citing fatigue. Would the Board or any of the IPL franchises allow such leeway to one of its star players if he wished to skip an IPL or Champions League tournament on the same grounds? For that matter, would any player dare risk such a move, considering the huge loss of earnings that would entail?

Yet the 'Indian' team now has to grapple with its top players missing out on international cricket due to injuries picked up in the IPL. And the Board, the IPL management, and its band of embedded journalists desperately initiate 'Operation Cover-up' whenever this occurs.

The Champions League begins three days after the end of the Champions Trophy; next year's World T20 begins five days after the end of IPL Season III. This despite Kirsten's plea to give more time for rest and recuperation. The BCCI has not slotted in a single T20 International for 'their' team between the last World T20 held in June and the next in April-May 2010. They believe IPL III is preparation enough.

The captain and coach disagree. But then, who cares for 'Indian' cricket? Certainly not the BCCI.

□

(The New Indian Express, 8/10/09)

Sachin Tendulkar at 20

The year 2009 marked the 20th anniversary of Sachin Tendulkar's entry into international cricket. Here I celebrate his achievements.

India was a very different place from what it is today when Sachin Tendulkar stepped into the cauldron of international cricket in Pakistan 20 years ago.

Events rapidly followed that debut in November 1989 in all of which Tendulkar was not a direct catalyst. But his presence at the centre of these massive changes in both India and the game of cricket was like the planets lining up in the rare celestial occurrence called planetary alignment.

India's was a closed economy two decades back. But then in 1991, current Prime Minister and then Finance Minister Manmohan Singh ushered in the opening of India's markets to the world. The same year Rupert Murdoch planted his electronic footprint in India with the arrival of his STAR TV satellite channels.

Today every conceivable luxury brand has a presence in India. And the Indian viewer has a choice of well over 200 channels including dozens of 24x7 news channels in dozens of languages including English.

After making an immediate impression as a baby-faced 16-year-old in Pakistan, Tendulkar then captured the hearts of the cricket world in 1990 when he became the youngest to score a Test century on English soil.

A year later he repeated the feat at Sydney and Perth leading Australian captain Allan Border to exclaim: "If he can play like this at 18, I shudder to think what he will be like at 25."

The seemingly endless saga of centuries had begun and 20 years later it shows no signs of abating.

When in 1995 Tendulkar signed a multi-million dollar endorsement deal with the late Mark Mascarenhas, he led another revolution, that of the super-rich cricketer. The ripple effect of that deal can be seen today in the vast sums of money being splurged on the Indian Premier League. If the Indian market drives the cricket world's economy, a major reason for that is Tendulkar's phenomenal success.

Tendulkar is arguably cricket's first $100 million man and no doubt the first of many more to follow. Yet, after hundreds of matches and enough money to last his family generations, he still retains the enthusiasm of a teenager when he steps onto the field. "Every morning I just can't wait to get out on the park", he said in a recent interview marking his 20th anniversary.

When I got down to writing the first major biography of Tendulkar in late 2001, I was struck by the fact that over and above his major batting feats, there was not a speck of dirt on his image.

Indians like their sporting heroes to be squeaky clean, family oriented and upholding traditional middle class values. Tendulkar ticks all these boxes, even though his marriage at the age of 22 raised some eyebrows—it was after all a 'love marriage' to an older career woman who was half-English to boot.

As for his upbringing, the Tendulkar family was solidly middle class. The fact that his professor-father allowed him to discontinue his education before graduation was considered rather radical for the time though.

When Tendulkar was chosen for that maiden tour of Pakistan, one of the selectors asked: "what if he fails?" Chief selector Naren

Tamhane's response—"Gentlemen, Sachin Tendulkar never fails"—has become part of Indian cricket folkore.

But if there has been one area where he has indeed failed it is with the captaincy. Two stints—1996 to 1998 and 1999 to 2000—both ended in failure, bitter recriminations and even tears. Even two years as captain of the richest franchise in the IPL, Mumbai Indians has been a major disappointment.

Though much of the cricket world and all of India had proclaimed him to be the best batsman in the world, it took the ringing endorsement of the greatest of them all, Sir Don Bradman to place the final seal of approval on the batting maestro. In 1996 Sir Don anointed him as his spiritual heir and when 'Bradman's Best' was released posthumously in 2001, Tendulkar was the only contemporary player in his all-time XII.

All those runs, all that wealth, all those awards and all that fame…And yet, it took a tragedy of staggering proportions to bring out the best in Tendulkar. When the English team returned to India just weeks after the horror of the terrorist attack on Mumbai in November last year, Tendulkar's match winning century in the Chennai Test made it more than just a game. It was a moment of national joy and vindication. It was as if the Indian spirit had proven its resilience.

It brought to mind what poet and columnist CP Surendran had written so poignantly of the little master some years back. Every time he walks to the wicket "a whole nation, tatters and all, marches with him to the battle arena. A pauper people pleading for relief, remission from the lifelong anxiety of being Indian…seeking a moment's liberation from their India-bondage through the exhilarating grace of one accidental bat."

It is doubtful if cricket will ever see his like again.

□

(Jonathan Agnew's Cricket Year 2009, published by A & C Black)

Jingoism Reaches New Heights in IPL Avatar

The ominous warning of Lalit Modi's intentions began to ring true within weeks of the publication of this article.

The Indian Premier League has become the latest chest-thumping vehicle for Indian Netizens both at home and abroad.

Any non-Indian critic of the annual jamboree now into its third year is immediately dubbed a racist. Any Indian critic is branded a traitor. Jingoism has found a new vehicle in India and the rest of the cricket world is told to dance to its tune or take a hike.

How a domestic cricket league with a smattering of international players came to this pass is entirely due to the massive PR machine cranked out by Lalit Kumar Modi and his merry band of Bollywood stars, fat-cat businessmen, ex-players and journalists, all with a vested financial interest in singing from the same hymn sheet.

The clamour for the International Cricket Council to create a 'window' free of international cricket for the six weeks of the IPL in summer and the two weeks of the Champions League in winter is growing ever louder. But assuming the ICC succumbs to such pressure and gives Modi what he wants, will he settle for that? That looks increasingly unlikely.

The man who snatched the idea for the Twenty-20 franchise league format from the now-defunct 'rebel' Indian Cricket League (ICL)—crushed by the all-powerful Board of Control for Cricket in India—is a businessman with a massive ego, ferocious appetite for power and contempt for nation v. nation cricket which he thinly veils in cleverly released statements.

Make no mistake—Modi and the IPL's ultimate target is not six or eight weeks in the calendar. The recent deals struck by the Rajasthan Royals franchise with teams from England, South Africa and the West Indies is just the first step. The franchise owners will never be satisfied with being in the spotlight for just six to eight weeks a year. Their target, hand-in-glove with Modi is to expand their operations worldwide and year-round. The Board of Control for Cricket in India too is complicit in this scheme of things.

World cricket domination is in Modi's sights and it is the Indian cricket public who will decide whether he gets what he desires or has his ambitious plans thwarted.

But there are bumps on the superhighway and the biggest was revealed in Mumbai where the auction for two new franchises for IPL IV collapsed on Modi like a warm soufflé.

Modi's enormous appetite created indigestion for the big bosses of the BCCI who are the IPL's parent body. Bidders stayed away, put off by the ridiculous terms and conditions set by Modi.

The Ravindra Jadeja scandal also proves that the players are helpless—albeit richly paid—pawns. The real power vests with the Commissioner and the owners which in a couple of cases is one and the same.

For the owners, these players, many of them national icons, are the ultimate status symbols Flaunted much like the latest Gucci handbag or Manolo Blahnik shoes; they have been turned into trophy players for the owners and dutifully walk a few steps behind their new masters.

While 60 matches are being played this year, next year the number jumps to 94 with two new franchises being added. Will the

Indian cricket-mad public continue to lap up this TV reality show or will they too suffer from indigestion? If the experiment does indeed succeed, you can be sure more and more franchises will be added over the years. Greed knows no boundaries.

For senior cricketers the IPL is like a gilt-edged Voluntary Retirement Scheme. Why spend the year traveling the cricket world to play for your country when you can take home 10 times the money playing hit-and-giggle cricket for a few weeks? This has led to a spate of retirements from international cricketers who want to conserve their energies for IPL which takes little out of their bodies, but adds plenty to their bank accounts.

For the new generation, the temptations are irresistible. Why slog and sweat it out for the handful of places in the national or even state side when you can make a tidy packet bowling four overs or batting for a few more? The route to riches has never been easier.

Given these choices, one can hardly blame the cricketers. It is the authorities who have created this money-fuelled monster that has upturned a value system going back over a century in a matter of three years.

So what if the IPL is creating a generation of half-baked cricketers who fail at the international cricket? If Modi has his way, such cricket will anyway be defunct. And make no mistake, there is no place for both formats in the increasingly crowded cricket calendar.

South Africa in 2008 was just the first step. Canada and the United States beckon. In five years time will international cricket be replaced by IPL-backed franchises traveling round the world with Modi the ringmaster cracking the whip? The toothless ICC can only watch helplessly as it is increasingly rendered irrelevant.

It is the Indian fan alone who will ultimately decide world cricket's fate. Hang on for the ride.

□

(The New Indian Express, 18/3/10)

200 and Counting

The cricket world was awe-struck when Sachin Tendulkar became the first man to score a double century in an ODI.

After close to 3,000 One-day Internationals matches and nearly 40 years, the 200-barrier was finally breached by Sachin Tendulkar with his unbeaten double ton against South Africa at Gwalior's Captain Roop Singh stadium in February.

Now approaching his 37th birthday and in his 21st year of international cricket, Tendulkar had come close on at least three previous occasions.

So what took so long for the barrier to fall? Indeed, how come Tendulkar had to wait till the twilight of his career before he got to the magical mark in his 442nd match?

This is not to take anything away from the phenomenal feat which can be compared with West Indian legend Brian Lara becoming the first to score 400 in a Test match back in 2004.

But Lara's record, against Australia at St. John's, Antigua came in nearly 1,300 matches fewer than Tendulkar's feat (1,696th Test match against the 2,962nd ODI). This when ODI team totals have crossed the 400-run mark on nine occasions in the last four years alone.

It was the unknown Zimbabwean Charles Coventry who raised eyebrows last August when he came agonizingly close to the mark against Bangladesh at Harare. If not for losing the strike for most of the final over of the innings, he would surely have got those six runs he needed to reach 200.

Instead, he was left stranded on 194 not out and to add salt to his wounds, Zimbabwe were beaten by four wickets! Coventry thus drew level with Pakistan opener Saeed Anwar's record score against India at Chennai in 1997.

Coventry's innings was shrugged off as it came against the weak Bangladesh bowling attack.

But then, how come Tendulkar in 12 ODI's has managed just one century against Bangladesh? It was all a mystery and a puzzle. But that was finally unraveled at Gwalior and the record set straight. In Tendulkar's own words: "It [the record] was like solving a jigsaw puzzle. You begin solving it and then everything falls into place."

In Anwar's case, the left-hander began suffering from cramps in the sweltering Chennai heat by the time he had reached 75 in the Independence Cup tournament in May 1997.

Ironically it was Tendulkar who was captaining India at the time and he agreed to Anwar's request for a 'runner'. Tendulkar was accused of being soft as he was well within his rights in turning down the request. Anwar thus got the bulk of his runs with the swift-footed Shahid Afridi doing the hard yards for him.

Tendulkar too began to cramp up as he approached the 190 mark at Gwalior. But batting with a 'runner' can be a fraught situation due to mix-ups in calling between the three batsmen on the field and Tendulkar soldiered on alone. A wise decision as he had to scamper one's and two's towards the end.

It was just four months earlier at Hyderabad that Tendulkar appeared to be cruising to 200 even as India looked to chase down Australia's mammoth 350 for four.

He got to his century at Hyderabad from 81 balls and his 150 from 122 as against 90 and 118 at Gwalior.

But after a flawless innings, Tendulkar was out for 175 in the 47th over and India fell short of victory by just three runs.

It makes a fascinating study to look back at the progression to the record since the first ODI was played at Melbourne between England and Australia back in January 1971.

England opener Dennis Amiss recorded the first ODI century in just the second match a year later against Australia at Manchester. And it was in the first World Cup in 1975 that New Zealand opener Glenn Turner became the first batsman to cross 150 with his 171 not out against minnows East Africa at Birmingham.

That stood as the highest score for eight years and nearly 200 matches before Kapil Dev established himself as the new record holder with his epochal 175 not out against Zimbabwe at Tunbridge Wells in the 1983 Prudential World Cup which India stunned the world by going onto win. Now 27 years later the record has returned to India.

One-day cricket has changed immensely since those early days. The overs have been reduced from 60 in the first three World Cups to 50 since 1987. Today more than ever though it is a batsman's game, particularly since the advent of Twenty-20 cricket. Both the equipment and laws have seen drastic changes, all to the batsman's benefit.

It must be remembered that it was not till the late 70s that international cricket saw the advent of the helmet. Till then, in the words of former England captain Mike Atherton, potentially every ball could have been the last he would ever face in his life for a batsman against a rampaging fast bowler who aimed for the batsman's head almost as often as his stumps.

Apart from the helmet and all the other protective gear—which West Indian legends Sir Viv Richards and Sir Garry Sobers contemptuously refer to as 'armour'—the biggest change has been in the advances made in bat manufacturing. With these massive weapons in their hands and helmets and chest and elbow guards as their shields, batsmen today are in a position to play audacious shots without fear of physical harm and even mishits and edges sail over the boundary line.

As if that were not enough to make the bowler's life a misery, how about the ridiculous 'free-hit' rule first introduced in the T-20 version and now in ODIs as well? The bowlers are reduced to virtual canon fodder in today's limited overs game where they are also constrained by restrictive no-ball rules governing the height of the delivery and tough rulings on wides. The Powerplays introduced a few years back has made life that much easier for batsmen and the pendulum has now swung decisively their way.

Pitches in the Asian sub-continent have always favoured the batting side, more so in ODIs. It is no coincidence that four of the 10 highest ODI totals have come in India and Sri Lanka. With the ball barely rising waist high on these dead tracks, a batsman of Tendulkar's calibre gets out more often due to his own error of judgment rather than any skills on the part of the bowler.

But apart from the use of helmets, perhaps the biggest gain for batsmen has been the reduction in the size of the boundary. This change was brought about by the advent of the Indian Premier League in 2008 and the demand from sponsors and spectators for more and more big hits.

At Gwalior it appeared the boundary was barely 60 yards, a ridiculously short distance more suited for a schools match rather than an international. It is no surprise there were as many as 15 sixes in the match including three by Tendulkar and 71 boundaries to boot. Pity the poor bowler!

Despite all that, it takes tremendous technique, temperament and fitness to bat all 50 overs, something Tendulkar had managed on just one previous occasion when he scored 186 not out against New Zealand at Hyderabad back in 1999.

After a slump in form, at least by his own lofty standards between 2002 to 2006, the last calendar year was Tendulkar's finest with 1,636 runs including five hundreds and six fifties from 35 ODIs.

Last year included yet another occasion where the double century was his for the taking. It was at Christchurch last March where the Kiwi bowlers felt the full might of his batting.

It was only an injury that forced him to retire hurt on 163 with five overs to go that probably thwarted his bid and saw him having to wait another 11 months for the magical moment, appropriately enough on Indian soil in front of his adoring fans.

Before Gwalior, most experts felt it would be the West Indian Chris Gayle, Sri Lanka's Tillakaratne Dilshan or Virender Sehwag who would get there first.

Instead it was Sehwag who was awe-struck by the Little Master's "ridiculous ease" of batting at Gwalior that saw him ascend to the summit first.

The best news for Indian cricket is that Tendulkar is back to full fitness after a shocking spate of injuries starting in 1999 that struck almost every part of his body and was a major cause for his slump.

The biggest prize that awaits is the World Cup to be staged jointly by India, Sri Lanka and Bangladesh in 12 months time. For all his personal landmarks, this is one goal that has eluded Tendulkar and he makes no secret of his hunger for cricket's Holy Grail.

The 2011 World Cup may also be his swansong in national colours. For the sake of Indian cricket, it would be a perfect symmetry if Tendulkar were to bow out with his hands clasping the World Cup.

□

(Namaskaar, April 2010)

Helmets and Balance of Power in Cricket

The evolution of the batting helmet has been a trend I have followed with great interest.

More than any change in law or any other piece of equipment, including hi-tech bats, it is the use of the helmet that has inexorably swung the balance of power towards the batsman in modern-day cricket.

Would the audacious shots unveiled by Brendon McCullum or Tillakaratne Dilshan particularly in T-20 cricket been possible without this essential piece of facial and skull protection? Highly doubtful.

West Indian legend Sir Garfield Sobers who did not even wear a thigh-guard during his glittering career weighed in on the debate—first articulated by Sir Vivian Richards—during a recent visit to India.

No surprise that Sir Garry rated India's ace opener Sunil Gavaskar as the best of his generation for taking on the battery of West Indian quicks without the benefit of a helmet.

Going by Sir Viv's attack on "pampered" modern batsmen with their helmets and body armour, cricket has become a game for sissies since the helmets were first introduced in the late 70s.

Richards was famous for striding out with the West Indies

crimson cap perched imperiously on his head and proceeding to swat fast bowlers all over the ground. The pace of Dennis Lillee and Jeff Thomson briefly rattled him Down Under in 1975-76. But a few sessions with a sports shrink and he was a new man.

Former England captain Mike Atherton while assessing the career of Sachin Tendulkar ruffled feathers when he claimed it would be "demeaning" to the masters of old to be compared to the Indian champion for one simple reason—Tendulkar batted throughout his career with a helmet.

Helmets were practically unheard of till Australia's Graham Yallop used one for the first time in the Bridgetown Test in March 1978.

As Atherton put it so succinctly: "...those former greats stood at the crease in the knowledge that their next ball could be their last."

While Yallop was the first to use the helmet in a Test match, it was England opener Dennis Amiss who first made jaws drop with his unique protective gear in the first season of Kerrry Packer's rebel World Series Cricket.

It did not take long for many others to follow which is hardly surprising considering the season had barely begun when David Hookes had his jaw broken while attempting to hook Andy Roberts at the Sydney Showground in December 1977.

Roberts led a galaxy of fast bowling demons who were given their full rein in WSC with its emphasis on pace, pace and more pace.

Backing him up were the formidable and fearsome trio of West Indian trio of Michael Holding, Colin Croft and Joel Garner.

Add to that the express pace of Imran Khan, Garth Le Roux, Lillee, Thomson and Len Pascoe and their unlimited usage of the short ball and one can understand why the batsmen of WSC feared for their lives and careers.

Early batting headgear was nothing but motorcycle crash helmets and so cumbersome were they that they hampered the movement of batsmen and their hearing as well. The result was a spate of run outs.

Post-Packer, the West Indian fast bowling greats were joined by perhaps the greatest of them all, Malcolm Marshall and still there were no strict guidelines for umpires to restrict intimidation.

Helmets were by now common usage but they evolved from the motorcycle variety to a slightly more streamlined style. The visor was still in usage but this impeded the vision of batsmen as it tended to get smudged and fogged over.

By the 90s the helmet minus any facial protection appeared with only the cranium covered. This resulted in bloody noses and facial injuries, notably to Mike Gatting in the West Indies in 1986 at the hands of Marshall and Sachin Tendulkar by Waqar Younis on his first tour in Pakistan in 1989.

By the 2000s, cricket had adapted the American gridiron football helmet with face grille protection and this has now become standard usage for batsmen, fielders and even wicket-keepers standing up to spinners.

Richards' strong views on modern batsmen re-opened the debate on the pre-helmet era and the courage batsmen of yore needed. But it was somehow forgotten by both Richards and Atherton that the flamboyant West Indian strokemaker was not the last batsman to complete his career without ever resorting to the helmet.

Credit should also be given to Gavaskar, the first to reach 10,000 Test runs. And it took Sobers to point this out.

Gavaskar made his debut in 1971 in the West Indies with a world record 774 runs in his first series when Sobers was the opposing captain. He scored 13 centuries against Roberts, Holding and co. in 27 Tests at the outstanding average of 65.45. No one before or since has come close to these marks.

It was not till the 1983-84 season that Gavaskar began to wear a fiberglass skull protector under his hat, something England captain Mike Brearley experimented with in 1976 against the West Indies. But right till his retirement in 1987, Gavaskar eschewed the helmet.

The pioneer in this regard was another Englishman, Patsy Hendren who wore a rubber head protector under his cap against the West Indian fast bowlers Learie Constantine and Manny Martindale way back in 1933.

The big question is: would Richards have been strutting helmet-less around the cricket world, hooking bowlers out of the ground and scoring tons of runs if he had to face his own fast bowlers from the Caribbean islands?

That is something we will never know. But in West Indies domestic cricket, his record is quite ordinary. Playing first for the Combined Leeward and Windward Islands and then for the Leeward Islands, Richards recorded nine centuries in 54 matches (90 innings). This reflects poorly against his Test record of 24 hundreds in 121 matches and 182 innings.

Even in county cricket while playing first for Somerset and then Glamorgan, his compatriots would take great glee in picking up his wicket on the domestic English circuit.

What is remarkable is that no professional cricketer was killed in the pre-helmet era. The worst injuries were to India's captain Nari Contractor on the 1962 tour of the West Indies at the hands of Charlie Griffith and New Zealand's Ewen Chatfield after being struck by the gentler pace of England's Peter Lever at Auckland in 1975.

Contractor's international career was ended by the blow and when I spoke to him on the 40th anniversary of the near-tragic incident he freely admitted he would have been happy to wear a helmet had they been around in his time.

Despite all this protection, if batsmen get hit even today and sometimes suffer serious injury it is no doubt because complacency has set in and reflexes have slowed perhaps due to the extra weight on the head and neck region.

Indeed, some of the injuries of the helmet era have been quite horrific. Some even feel that more batsmen have been hit on the head and the face in the helmet era than before. Obviously even a helmet cannot afford 100 per cent safety if the bowler is super-fast and accurate and the batsman's technique and reflexes are faulty.

Then again with the evolution of the cricket bat and with the modern batsman swathed in protective gear, the decline of the bowler has been more pronounced in the last decade than any since the likes of Bill Ponsford, Stan McCabe, Don Bradman and Wally Hammond plundered runs galore in the 1930s.

The advent of Twenty-20 cricket, flat pitches and shorter boundaries all points to batsmen continuing their domination in the new decade.

□

(DreamCricket.com, 14/5/10)

Make Way for The Ladies

Women's sports in India has come a long way from the days of competing in salwar-kameez and saris.

Saina Nehwal's rise to the top of the world badminton rankings is yet another landmark in the history of Indian sportswomen and comes on the 40th anniversary of their first significant international achievement.

It was at the 1970 Asian Games in Bangkok that Kanwaljit Sandhu won the first international gold medal for an Indian sportswoman in the 400 metres.

This was followed by the PT Usha era of the 1980s while this decade saw the emergence of Sania Mirza and world amateur boxing champion MC Mary Kom.

It was an uphill struggle for sportswomen from the time of independence till the 60s with just a handful of sports like tennis, badminton, table tennis, athletics and hockey open to them.

The tiny Parsi and Anglo-Indian communities led the way in those early years and it was in the matter of clothing that sportswomen in India saw their progress stifled.

A girl seen in public in shorts or skirts was considered scandalous and it was a common sight to see them competing in *salwar-kameez* and even *saris.*

Among the early stars were Roshan Mistry (a Parsi), 100m. silver medalist in the first Asian Games in Delhi in 1951 and Stephie D'Souza, the first woman to receive the Arjuna Award in 1963.

D'Souza was part of the relay team that won gold in the 4x100m. at the 1954 Asian Games and also represented India in hockey.

Geeta Zutshi also struck gold in the 800 metres in the 1978 Asian Games. But by now the Kerala era in women's athletics was beginning to unfold. This was thanks to the sports hostel concept in the state where the government funded the education and training of promising young athletes.

When the Asian Games returned to New Delhi in 1982, MD Valsamma was one of the stars with her gold in the 400 metres hurdles. The Indian women's hockey team also made up for the ignominy suffered by the men who were trounced 7-1 in the final by Pakistan.

Angel Mary Joseph, Valsamma, Usha and Shiny Abraham were at the forefront of the Kerala surge while Karnataka produced the first glamour girls of Indian sport in Ashwini Nachappa, Reeth Abraham and Vandana Rao. This trio could not match the medal winning feats of their Kerala counterparts but captured the media glare with their looks and daring outfits.

Usha won silver in the 100 and 200 m. in 1982. For the rest of the decade there was no one to challenge her supremacy in Asia.

But Usha's greatest—and saddest—moment came at the 1984 Los Angeles Olympics when she became the first Indian woman to reach an Olympics track and field final in the 400 metres hurdles and was edged into fourth place.

Since then only Anju Bobby George has matched Usha's feat when she reached the final of the women's long jump in the 2004 Olympics having the previous year won silver in the world championship at Paris. That remains the lone medal won by an Indian athlete, male of female, at the world event.

By 1986 Usha was unstoppable. The Seoul Asian Games was an all-time low for Indian sport as it managed to bag just five gold medals. Four were won by Usha (plus one silver), the fifth in kabaddi.

The rapid strides shown by women on the sporting front saw them shift their focus from the 1990s onwards to the traditionally masculine preserves of weightlifting, boxing and wrestling.

Karnam Malleswari and Kunjarani Devi bagged international weightlifting medals galore and when Malleswari won the bronze in the 69kg division at the Sydney Olympics she set yet another landmark—the first Olympic medal for an Indian woman.

Sania Mirza burst on the scene spectacularly in 2005 by rising up the world tennis rankings while at the same time turning heads and raising eyebrows.

Sania broke down barriers of gender and religion and had the world media turning its attention to India. Her glam appeal meant endorsement deals for the Hyderabadi heartthrob was now rivaling those of India's top cricketers.

But the shift from the back sports pages to the front news pages and then to the page three glamour pages—combined with injuries and various controversies—saw Mirza lose focus, rankings and popularity. Today she is reduced to an also-ran on the world tennis circuit.

Her comet-like career though has sent out warning signs to Saina who no doubt has learnt some important life lessons from her fellow-Hyderabadi's rapid rise and equally sudden fall.

In sports as varied as archery, shooting, chess—Koneru Humpy is ranked world number two—to boxing where MC Mary Kom is the four-time amateur world champion in the 46 kg category, women have made impressive strides since Kanwaljit Sandhu's breakthrough feat four decades back.

Today, thanks to the courageous pioneers who defied the oppressive constraints of a patriarchal society, the sky is the limit for women's sports in India. The forthcoming Commonwealth Games in New Delhi and the 2012 Olympics in London should see this movement reach its pinnacle and bring more glory to Indian sports.

□

(Hindustan Times, 30/6/10)

Bibliography

List of books:

1. ***Indian Table Tennis Yearbook 1992*** (The Marine Sports, Bombay)
2. ***The Story of World Cup Cricket 1996*** (Konark Publishers, New Delhi)
3. ***The Story of World Cup Cricket 1999*** (Update; Konark)
4. ***Great One-day Internationals*** (1999; Orient Longman, Hyderabad)
5. ***Great Indian Olympians 2000*** (Co-authored with K. Arumugam; Thambi Thendril Publications, New Delhi)
6. ***Sachin: The Story of the World's Greatest Batsman*** (2002; Penguin India)
7. ***Sourav: A Biography*** (2003; Penguin India)
8. ***Icons From the World of Sports*** (2003; Puffin Books)
9. ***Great Indian Olympians 2004*** (Revised and updated edition. Co-authored with K. Arumugam; Field Hockey Publications, New Delhi)
10. ***The A-Z of Sachin Tendulkar*** (2005; UBS Publications, New Delhi)
11. ***The Penguin Book of Cricket Lists*** (2007; Penguin India)
12. ***Captain Cool: The MS Dhoni Story*** (2008; Westland Publishers, Chennai)
13. ***Sachin: The Story of the World's Greatest Batsman*** (2010; Revised and updated edition; Penguin India)

Indian Language Translations

Sachin Tendulkar: The Story of the World's Greatest Batsman

In Hindi: *Master Blaster Tendulkar* (Prabhat Prakashan, New Delhi, 2004)

In Gujarati: *Master Blaster Sachin Tendulkar* (RR Sheth and Co, Mumbai and Ahmedabad, 2005)

Sourav Ganguly: A Biography

In Hindi: *Bengal Tiger Ganguly* (Prabhat Prakashan, 2004)

In Gujarati: *Bengal Tiger Ganguly* (RR Sheth and Co, Mumbai and Ahmedabad, 2005)

Icons from the World of Sports

In Telugu: *Kreeda Rangamlo Pratibha Moorthulu* (Alakananda Pracharanulu, Vijaywada, 2005)

Captain Cool: The MS Dhoni Story

In Hindi: *Captain Cool: Mahendra Singh Dhoni Ki Kahani* (Westland Ltd, Chennai, 2008)

In Tamil: *Adhiradi Dhoni! MS Dhoniyin Kadhai* (Westland Ltd, Chennai, 2008)

In Marathi: *Captain Cool: Mahendra Singh Dhonichi Yashogatha* (Westland Ltd, Chennai, 2008)

Great Indian Olympians

In Hindi ; Mahaan Bharaitya Olympic Khiladi (Satsahitya Prakashan 2010)

As contributor

Indian Cricket 1984 (uncredited)

The Best of Expressport 1985

The Best of Expressport 1986

Penguin Test Match Year 1996-97

The New Ball (The Best New Cricket Writing—1999) Vol. IV: Imperial Bedrooms

The New Ball (The Best New Cricket Writing—2002) Vol. VII: Mind Games

Indian Cricket: No Balls (2002; satire from jaalmag.com)

Who's Who on Indian Stamps (2004)

Wisden Cricketers' Almanack 2005 (photo only)

C and G Cricket Yearbook 2005

C and G Cricket Yearbook 2006

Cricket Year 2007

India Extraordinaire: 60 Years, 60 Luminaries (2007; Uncredited)

Jonathan Agnew's Cricket Year 2008

Jonathan Agnew's Cricket Year 2009

Jonathan Agnew's Cricket Year 2010

Limca Book of Records (numerous editions)

Career Graph

Freelancing 1980-82

Indian Express, Madras (1982-91)

New Delhi:

The Pioneer (1991-93)

Asian Age (1993-94)

Financial Express (1994-95)

Outlook (1995-96)

NDTV (1996-2000)

indya.com (2000-01)

GE Features syndication/freelancing (2001 onwards)

□□□